STUDENTS ACROSS AMERICA SPEAK OUT!

"Too many people talk about being politically correct without doing anything. They don't realize it's the little changes in our everyday activities, like what products we buy, that really count."

GILLIAN CHI, 18
New York

"I believe that social responsibility begins with one person."

DAVID LYONS, 14
New York

"We need to take charge of our future and get involved with these companies, keep our eye on them. We are the only ones who can make a difference in what's going on in our world."

LISA SHILVOCK, 19
Texas

"It is all of our jobs to keep the world healthy."

LATIMER SHUI, 17
New York

"I feel equal rights are very important, just like a company being truthful is. If a company was lying, I'd definitely change brands! I also feel it's important to preserve the environment."

BRANDI BRUNS, 14
Ohio

STUDENTS SHOPPING FOR A BETTER WORLD

ROBIN DELLABOUGH *project director*
BEN HOLLISTER *researcher*
ALICE TEPPER MARLIN *executive director*
EMILY SWAAB *research director*

with JONATHAN ROSE *and* ROSALYN WILL

Preface by Teresa Heinz

CEP
COUNCIL ON ECONOMIC PRIORITIES

Council on Economic Priorities, Inc.
BALLANTINE BOOKS • NEW YORK

ACKNOWLEDGMENTS

The Council on Economic Priorities would like to thank everyone who made this book possible through financial support, hard work, advice, or friendship. Without the Teresa and H. John Heinz III Fund of the Heinz Family Foundation, the Mary Reynolds Babcock Foundation, and the Marie C. and Joseph C. Wilson Foundation, there would be no book at all. Without research interns David Aron, Sara Eichler, Dianne Gobin, Mark Gothard, Amy Ickowitz, Hakeem Jeffries, Stephen Kalland, Matthew Psichoulas, Ian Reifowitz, Fumiyo Tanaka, Tina Verdon, Marc Williams, and Elizabeth Wong, there would be less content. Without Dean Pappalardo and Maureen O'Brien, there would be no design. Thanks also to all our advisers, young and old, and to the criteria committee of CEP's board of directors. (See page 247 for a complete list.) Miscellaneous but heartfelt thanks to Thomas Roemer, Bobby Ballard, Matt Nicodemus, Marlitt Dellabough, and Jon, Joel, and Flynn Berry.

All royalties from the sale of this book go to the Council on Economic Priorities, a non-profit research organization, to support further research on the social responsibility of corporations.

 Published in the United States of America by Ballantine Books, a division of Random House, Inc., New York, and simultaneously in Canada by Random House of Canada Limited, Toronto.

CEP
COUNCIL ON ECONOMIC PRIORITIES

Council on Economic Priorities, Inc.
30 Irving Place, New York, NY 10003
212-420-1133

Library of Congress Catalog Card Number: 93-90179

ISBN 0-345-37333-2

This edition is published by arrangement with the Council on Economic Priorities, Inc.

Manufactured in the United States of America

First Ballantine Books Edition: September 1993

Table of Contents

PREFACE

People often ask me if my childhood in Africa was dangerous. It was if you didn't respect the rules of nature. We learned not to go to the ocean or the river in the morning or evening when animals come to feed or to drink. We learned to conserve, reuse, and save manufactured things because they were expensive and hard to get, whether cans, bottles, or cloth. We learned early a respect for nature and its rules—it meant survival in the wilderness. There was a natural order, and if you paid attention, you were safe.

Today, in our industrialized, urbanized communities, there are few clear rules. Modern civilization has meant a better life for many. But with this civilization has come environmental threats and a more complex society. You probably already know about many of these problems. They are big and complicated and they touch each of us.

When I talk with young people about these problems, many question whether one person can make a difference. There is a feeling of frustration that what is going on today is a result of the decisions made by past generations.

Students Shopping for a Better World promotes action—steps every individual can take to improve our world. There are immense opportunities for each of us to do good, lasting, important work. And you don't have to wait until you have graduated from high school or college or started a career before you can begin to make change. You can begin to make a better world right now.

Students Shopping for a Better World is a do-it-yourself guide on how to exercise your power as a consumer to protect the environment, promote equal opportunities for women and minorities in the business world, prevent cruelty to animals, and reward corporations that act responsibly. This book gives you facts about the companies whose products you buy, an alternative to slick advertising hype. You can choose products made by companies whose policies and practices you support. Companies responsible for deforestation, toxic landfills, and polluted streams, for example, are companies whose products you may not want in your shopping bag. Buying products that are environmentally sound doesn't mean falling for every product with a green label.

Your imagination and energy is a valuable, and often overlooked, resource. You have the ability to create respect for nature and each other. Choices you make as a thoughtful consumer do have consequences. This does not excuse the companies that pollute or governments that fail to act, but let's really think about our own buying choices.

I happened to grow up in a real jungle. With the information provided in this book, you will be able to clear a path through the jungle we call the consumer marketplace. Our goal is to get companies to march to the same tune as their customers and understand the reasons we have for buying their products. Such consumer power will force responsible social and environmental behavior through economics—for a future we can all afford.

As my late husband, United States Senator John Heinz, said, standing on the steps of the Capitol on Earth Day 1990, "remember that green is magic...and the color of your money is green. Use your green magic as if the fate of our planet depends on the decisions you make every day. It does."

Teresa Heinz
Chairman, Heinz Family Philanthropies
Vice Chair, Environmental Defense Fund
September 1992

INTRODUCTION

What's the Big Idea?

WHAT'S THE BIG IDEA?

This book isn't really only about shopping. It's about everything.

It's about protecting the earth while we still have an earth left to protect. It's about making sure all human beings—women, men, children of any color—are treated equally and have equal opportunities. It's about preventing cruelty to animals. None of us exists alone. We live with each other, with nature, with the earth's creatures. Our lives are only as good as the lives of those around us. If we want the best possible world to live in, we need to look out for each other. That's called social responsibility: being aware of how each person influences the whole society.

Even more than responsibility, this book is about power. Your power. On these pages are tools you can use to create the kind of world you want—for today and for tomorrow. The ability to really change things is a gift. And you can give it to yourself.

So what does all that have to do with shopping? Look at it this way: every time you spend a dollar to buy something a company sells, you're sending a message. You're saying you not only like the company's clothes or candy or cassettes, you also support the way they do business. If you buy shampoo from a company that dumps toxic waste into rivers, you're saying that's acceptable. If you buy a pair of sneakers from a company that never hires minorities, you're saying that's okay with you.

Luckily, if you want, you can send a different message. You can seek out companies that are careful with the environment or that give women top management jobs or that try not to hurt animals. Then you're telling those companies to keep up the good work! That is what we call shopping for a better world.

THE INSIDE SCOOP

But how do you know which companies are doing terrific things for the world and which companies are in it just for the profits? Who rates high and who rates low? That's where this book comes in.

It would be impossible for any one individual to check up on every big company. Don't worry—we've done it for you. The Council on Economic Priorities research team has spent years investigating companies. We have them fill out detailed questionnaires. We scour newspapers and magazines. We check computer databases. We call experts around the country. Then we put all the information together in an easy-to-use guide.

So next time you're trying to decide between a Hershey's or a Nestle's candy bar, you can look them up in this book and see how they rate. Which one has a better track record in the environment? How about women's advancement or minority opportunity? Do they give to charity or test on animals? You can look up what's most important to you—and then make an informed decision about how to spend your money.

CHECK IT OUT

You could buy from a company like Esprit, for example. They make cool clothes. Better yet, they recycle excess scraps of cloth into reusable tote bags. All the paper, stationery, catalogs, and packaging they use is recycled. And they have 10 Eco Desks, special environmental departments to answer questions and coordinate their environmental efforts. The president of Esprit is a woman, more than half the officers and managers are women, and 20% are minorities. Plus, Esprit conducts no animal testing.

If you eat Kellogg's Corn Flakes for breakfast, you're supporting an outstanding employer for women and minorities. And talk about an environmentally aware company: not only does Kellogg have a waste reduction program, it has used recycled cardboard for cereal boxes since its founding in 1906! No wonder the Council on Economic Priorities gave Kellogg America's Corporate Conscience Award not once, but twice.

On the other hand, you (or your parents) may want to avoid filling up your gas tank with Marathon gas. The USX Corporation, which owns Marathon, lists no women or minorities on its board of directors. In 1991, the company agreed to pay $41.8 million to settle a 15-year-old case claiming discrimination against thousands of black job-seekers. USX has a history of dangerous environmental habits, including excess air pollution and worker safety violations.

ABOUT THIS BOOK

You can use this guide any way you want. You might turn directly to the fast-food ratings to see how your favorite fries score. You might prefer to start at the beginning and read straight through to the end. To help you decide, here's a short description of each section:

CHAPTER ONE: WHO CARES? YOU CARE!
Explains why we decided to write a book for teenagers, what you say about the issues, collectively speaking, and the strength of your consumer power.

CHAPTER TWO: SHOPPING FOR A BETTER ENVIRONMENT: THE GREEN SCENE.
Describes the state of the environment today, the hot issues, and what you can do about them.

CHAPTER THREE: ALL ABOUT ADVERTISING.
Tells how clever those ad agencies really are, how they get you to spend your dollars...not always with sense. How you can look at ads more critically.

CHAPTER FOUR: MONEY MATTERS.
Lists ways to be socially and financially responsible by using certain banks, credit cards, and credit unions.

CHAPTER FIVE: YOUR JOB/YOUR CAREER: FROM FAST FOOD TO FAST TRACK?
Provides things to look out for when you work, what to think about when considering what to do after high school and college.

CHAPTER SIX: SOCIAL ACTION: HAVE YOU GOT WHAT IT TAKES?
How to take social action. Five students tell how and why they made a difference. Plus how to start a recycling club at your school.

CHAPTER SEVEN: HOW TO USE THIS GUIDE.
Explains the rating system, rating issues, and how it's organized.

CHAPTER EIGHT: SHOPPING FOR YOUR FUTURE: RATINGS BY COMPANY.
The Honor Roll and Underachievers: the highest and lowest rated companies. Alphabetical list of large and small companies and their ratings.

CHAPTER NINE: SHOPPING FOR YOUR FUTURE: RATINGS BY PRODUCT.
Ratings by product category. This is the nitty gritty, the heart and soul of the book.

BREAKFAST FOOD
CLOTHING LABELS
CLOTHING STORES
COMPACT DISCS/AUDIO TAPES

CHAPTER 1

Who cares? You care!

WHO CARES? YOU CARE!

DEEP POCKETS

Why write a shopping guide especially for students? Because together you spend more than $80 billion a year—so deciding where you spend your money gives you a lot of power. Do you remember a few years ago when teenagers led a boycott of tuna companies? The companies were killing dolphins in the process of catching tuna. The boycott worked. The tuna companies responded by changing how they fished and protecting the dolphins.

''These issues are so important that we have to act now. By changing brands and boycotting, we might be able to make companies change their ways.''
Louisa Michaels, 12, California

That's one example of the kind of consumer power we're talking about. This book rates many of the companies whose products you buy, including jeans, sneakers, fast food, tapes, compact discs, gasoline, sports equipment, cosmetics, shampoo, condoms, toothpaste, school supplies and snacks.

Many large companies spend lots of money to get you to buy these products. They hire market researchers who are experts in figuring out what teenagers like—or even how to make you want things you didn't know you wanted. Why do you think Michael Jordan appears in ads for so many companies? The companies discovered he's one of the most popular sports heroes among your age group. So, along with other celebrities, such as Luke Perry, Paula Abdul, and Bo Jackson, his personality is used to get through to you. These corporations figure that when Michael talks, you walk...straight to the nearest store.

Another approach is to get in the door of your schools and colleges with free magazines, sample products, or even special "educational" programs. One prime example is Whittle Communications' Channel One. A current events video service, it's offered to schools free. But two minutes of each 12-minute segment is pure advertising—for candy, clothes, and other products that the sponsors count on you buying. (A study Whittle commissioned found that students had not learned anything educational from the program!)

Corporate America knows too that not only do you spend your own money, you influence your whole family's spending. More and more parents listen to their kids' advice on everything from which VCR to buy, to where to go on vacation, to which brand of cat food is best. In one survey, 34% of parents said they shop differently now because of something they learned from their children. So products that your parents actually pay for are being "sold" to you—for example, Club Med vacations, stereo systems, and single-dish microwave meals.

TEEN TALLY

Okay, so these companies are pretty good at getting you to spend your money. You can be equally sophisticated in how you spend it. Not only do you look for quality, good value, comfort, and taste—many of you already shop with a conscience. You're aware of what's happening in the world. And if you've read this far, you're probably ready to do whatever it takes—even switching from your favorite brands—to help improve your world.

''It is all of our jobs to keep the world healthy.''
Latimer Shui, 17, New York

"I believe very strongly in my power to create change by boycotting what I don't believe in and supporting what I do," says 17-year-old Jessica Tomkins of New Jersey. Adds Julie Miller, 15, of California: "If the company's record doesn't meet my standards, I would avoid its products as much as possible."

How do we know so much about you? Because we spent six months interviewing groups of students and analyzing hundreds of questionnaires you sent us. We heard from people aged 12 to 20; from California, Texas, Massachusetts, Indiana, Ohio, New York, Virginia, West Virginia, Maryland, South Dakota, Florida, and New Jersey; from city dwellers, suburbanites, and country kids; from blacks, whites, Native Americans, Asians, Hispanics, and Indians.

You told us some things about yourselves that we took for granted (70% eat fast food at least every two weeks)—and some we never would have guessed (93% buy shampoo at least once a month). When asked to name a famous person you'd like to be, a lot of you said you were happy being yourself!

Many of you also voiced a strong belief in teens as a group. According to Lisa Shilvock, 19, of Texas, "We need to take charge of our own future and get involved. We are the only ones who can make a difference in what's going on in the world."

''Too many people talk about being politically correct without doing anything. They don't realize it's the little changes in our everyday activities, like what products we buy, that really count.''
Gillian Chi, 18,
Brooklyn

When it comes to most important social issues, the environment tops nearly every teenager's list. In our survey, 75% consider the environment more important than any other single problem, and it rates much higher than any other issue. Why? "The environment is the most important issue," 13-year-old New Yorker Kyle Munigle says, "because hopefully most of us are going to be around for a pretty long time, and we want the earth to be good."

Next in order of importance to those we surveyed is equal opportunity for women and minorities, disclosure of information (how much a company tells the public), and animal welfare. As Karina Sang, 17, of the Bronx, puts it, "Some social issues concern me directly: equal job opportunities for women and minorities, since I am both." Adrian Jefferson, a 17-year-old from Staten Island, feels it's "important to know where a company stands, especially on social issues." And Leah Hickey, 16, of California, states, "If I found out that a product I regularly used had been tested on animals, I would not use the product."

Other areas of concern are whether companies violate child labor laws or contribute to their communities through donations or volunteer programs.

''I feel equal rights are very important, just like a company being truthful is important. If a company was lying, I'd definitely change brands!''
Brandi Bruns, 14,
Ohio

We tried to tell you as much as we could about company policies in these areas. Some issues we did not cover—gun control, AIDS, and drug abuse—are equally important to teenagers. They just didn't fit into corporate social responsibility very easily.

But there's no reason just to sit around and worry about problems. You can start small, think big, and change the world. As David Lyons, 14, of New York says, "I believe that social responsibility begins with one person."

Are you ready to begin?

CHAPTER 2

Shopping for a Better Environment

The Green Scene

SHOPPING FOR A BETTER ENVIRONMENT: THE GREEN SCENE

THE BIG PICTURE

If you live on this planet, chances are you've already heard a lot about the shape it's in: sick and getting worse fast. Here are the major symptoms:

GLOBAL WARMING

The "greenhouse effect," otherwise known as global warming, is heating up the earth. Our very survival is threatened. The six hottest years ever recorded in history occurred in the 1980s—and many people think the greenhouse effect is to blame. What's causing global warming?

There always have been gases in the atmosphere acting as a kind of blanket around the earth, which kept us warm enough to stay alive. But now some gases are making the blanket too thick. They include carbon dioxide, chlorofluorocarbons (CFCs), methane, and nitrous oxide. These gases come from cars, power plants, factories, air conditioners, refrigerators, plastics, aerosols, cattle, landfills, fossil fuels, fertilizers, and refineries—lots of things we believe we can't live without.

If global warming continues, we can expect droughts, floods, and famines.

OZONE LAYER DEPLETION

Ozone at ground level is toxic to humans. But ozone in the atmosphere is very important in shielding us from the sun's harmful ultraviolet rays—the kind that can give you a great tan, but also lead to skin cancer.

There is already a hole in the ozone layer over the Antarctic...as big as the entire United States. Scientists have discovered more gaps in the ozone layer over the northern hemisphere and the Arctic. The problem is worse than they had originally thought. CFCs, from air conditioners, refrigerators, solvents, plastic packaging, and foam insulation, are the main culprits.

In addition to contributing to skin cancer, ozone depletion threatens plant and ocean life. Ocean life, in turn, supplies 70% of the world's oxygen—what we need to stay alive!

POLLUTION

This country's industries, in just one recent year, dumped 22 billion pounds of toxic waste in our air, water, and soil—and it was all legal! Imagine how much pollution that waste caused. Air pollution alone is so severe that in many places people are warned not to go outdoors on particularly bad days. Our drinking water comes out of the ground. It only takes one gallon of gasoline seeping into the ground at a gas station to pollute almost a million gallons of drinking water.

Every day, we eat food grown in soil poisoned by pesticides. And much of the soil we used to grow food in has been lost through erosion or made unusable through contamination.

GARBAGE

Our garbage dumps, also called "landfills," are running out of room. We've already closed about **half** our landfills—and alternatives like burning garbage can be even worse for the environment.

The problem is that we make too much garbage. One American throws out 23 pounds of trash in **one week**, much more than the British, German, Japanese, Scandinavians, or French. That's why the Three R's—Reducing, Reusing, and Recycling—are so important.

DEFORESTATION

Trees are more than an appealing part of the landscape. They clean the air, affect rainfall, control erosion, and keep the climate in balance. They're pretty wonderful. You'd think we'd want to take care of them, right?

Yet most of the original forests in this country already have been cut down. And the tropical rainforests, home of more than half the world's plant and animal species, are systematically being destroyed. A chunk of rainforest as big as a football field is chopped down **every second**. Much of this destruction is done in order to make room for grazing cattle—the source of those burgers we consume at fast-food places. Most of us—and the folks who cut these trees—don't realize the rainforests produce much of our oxygen.

MULTIPLE CHOICE

Just how much time do we have before it's too late to save the earth? You may be surprised by the answer. In 1990 the Worldwatch Institute said the earth would face "economic and social ruin" by the year 2030 if we didn't start improving our environmental habits. By 1992, Worldwatch said the earth was dying already. We need to make a revolution, environmentally speaking, to prevent a disastrous end for our planet.

Environmental revolution might sound like too big a challenge. But every revolution begins with individuals making very small changes, either in how they think or how they act. All these changes add up. And it doesn't have to be all-consuming.

"Environmentalism is something I can do every day without stopping the rest of my life," explains 17-year-old Jeremy Burns. "It's something I can do while I'm doing other things."

ANOTHER DAY, A BETTER WAY

Here's how we can do it differently...and make a difference:

- Take shorter showers to save water and energy. Aim for under five minutes. You need to wash your hair only once to get it clean.

- Buy shampoo and other products with as little packaging as possible. Look for reusable or recyclable containers made of recycled materials.

- Use replaceable razors instead of disposables. Not only will you save room in overcrowded landfill, you'll save money too!

- Conserve energy at home. Use heaters and air conditioners efficiently. Turn off lights when you leave a room.

- Check the color of cardboard packaging—if a box is pure white, chances are it's not made from recycled materials. An earthy gray or brown is a good clue that it's been recycled. Even better is a "made from recycled materials" sign on the package.

- Avoid single-serving products. It's excess packaging. It's better to buy a big tin of cocoa, for example, than to use single-serving packets. Probably less loaded with preservatives and sugar, too.

- Every time a car uses one gallon of gasoline, it creates almost 20 pounds of carbon dioxide—the nasty chemical most responsible for global warming. When possible, walk, ride a bike, or use public transportation. Combine errands into one trip so you use the car efficiently. Try carpooling.

- Buy refillable pens and recycled pencils, notebooks, and paper. Check the back of notebooks for the recycled logo. If you have trouble finding recycled school supplies in your area, look up some great catalog companies that carry a whole line of recycled stationery.

- Packing your own lunch is a lot better for the environment than eating junk. But avoid plastic wrap and aluminum foil. Try using reusable containers. They keep sandwiches much fresher and neater anyway. Or reuse the bags and other packages that food you bought came in.

- If you do eat fast food, ask them to wrap it in paper rather than styrofoam. Try to use plates and cups you can wash and reuse.

- Although manufacturers claim you can recycle juice boxes, it's really not practical. It's a shame because juice boxes can be very convenient. But they're made of layers of paperboard, aluminum, and polyethylene that are hard to separate. It will take hundreds of years for a juice box to break down in a landfill. How about those reusable plastic squeeze bottles with the built-in straws? They look pretty cool, they're just as convenient, and they're the best for the earth.

- Recycle everything you possibly can...including cans! We hope your school or town already has a recycling program, which should make it super simple to recycle paper, magazines, newspapers, glass, even plastic bottles. If not, see Chapter Six for how to set up a recycling club at school. Meanwhile, get creative. Use the back sides of used paper for notes and scribbles. You can even staple together stacks of paper used only on one side to make your own notepads.

- Be aware that longboxes, the kind most compact discs used to come in, are a good example of bad packaging. The record companies thought longboxes would be easier to display and would discourage shoplifters. Some top musicians, like R.E.M. and Bonnie Raitt, have put pressure on recording companies to change this wastefulness. So most companies have switched over to more ecologically sound CD packaging by losing the longbox.

- Tell salespeople to hold the bag when shopping. Then put your purchases in a backpack, tote bag, string bag or whatever is your bag.

- If you and your friends all read the same magazines, why not try trading or sharing subscriptions? You'll save money and help the earth.

- Resist buying faddish clothing that will go out of style before it wears out. That's a waste of your money and the earth's resources. Instead, why not buy practical clothes made by a company with a good social record?

- Dry cleaning is not only expensive, it uses chemicals that can be harmful to you and the environment. Buy clothes made of natural fibers like cotton that can be washed. Even better, try Seventh Generation's GreenCotton clothes, made with a minimum use of energy and water and free of bleaches, dyes, and formaldehyde. (See page 138 for Seventh Generation's address.)

- It makes more sense to run washing machines, clothes dryers, and dishwashers only when they're full. You use less water, less detergent, less energy, and less time!

- Animals are part of our environment too. Avoid lotions and perfumes made from animal by-products. There's a good chance animals were killed just to produce such products.

- Same goes for buying jewelry, shoes, or other articles made from endangered species such as certain reptiles, elephants (ivory), or tortoises.

- If you want to look into the environmental history of a specific industry or company in more depth, check out CEP's Corporate Environmental Data Clearinghouse reports.

- Last but certainly not least: before you buy anything, check in this book to see whether there's another company that has a better track record in protecting the environment.

This is a pretty long list. No one expects you to be able to do it all. Even if you choose to make just one of the changes suggested here, you'd be helping the earth more than you realize.

CHAPTER 3

All About Advertising

ALL ABOUT ADVERTISING

Did you know that 10 cents of every dollar you spend pays for the company to advertise? American companies spend $130 billion a year just for advertising. Every day you're bombarded with hundreds of ads. Some you may notice. But even the ones you ignore have a way of sneaking into your subconscious, especially when companies are so clever about how and when they present ads. Consider the following examples:

- MAGAZINES—Fashion spreads in magazines are really ads for clothes. "Advertorials" seem like regular articles, until you read the fine print that says "advertisement." Magazines get advertisers to buy space by telling them in advance what each issue will contain.

- SCHOOLS—Companies give away free samples or "educational" posters with company logos on them, like Whittle Communications' poster on how the heart works with ads for fast food and candy alongside. Some educational videos contain regular commercials.

- MOVIES AND VIDEOS—Commercials for other movies appear before the main feature. Ads are shown at the beginning of videos. "Infomercials" are commercials that look like a news program, advice show, or game, but really promote a specific company or product. Specific brands are used in movies. Companies pay a lot for this kind of "product placement." Look for Miller beer in "Wayne's World" or Marlboros in "Superman II"—Philip Morris paid $42,000 for that "ad."

- MUSEUMS—Exhibits are sponsored by corporations and display corporate logos, such as Legos at the Smithsonian Institution in Washington, D.C.

• SPORTS EVENTS—Games, tournaments, and races are named after corporate sponsors. When it's a tobacco company, as in the Virginia Slims tennis tournament, it's really a killer! Tennis players, golfers, and race car drivers use equipment and wear clothes that sport logos and other advertising.

These are all examples of advertising, subtle and not so subtle. Maybe it's worth putting up with the ads—maybe not. The point is to realize how much your life is affected by the commercial world.

MADISON AVENUE MEETS MTV

How often have you said to your parents as they hold the remote control, ready to click off a commercial, "Don't turn it down, I like this one!"? It's little wonder that ads are often better than regular programs. Some of today's top movie and television directors, actors, and musicians are hired to produce 60 seconds of very high quality commercials, for very big money. Teenager Monica Seles earned over $1.5 million in 1991 playing tennis—and more than four times that amount endorsing Perrier, Matrix, and other products. Spike Lee has directed commercials for Nike and Levi. Bo Jackson and Michael Jordan, Madonna and Paula Abdul, Hammer and Ray Charles—they all help turn commercials into entertainment.

How do they do it? By using the same techniques music videos do. Images never stay on the screen for more than a few seconds. The pace is very fast, so the commercial seems exciting. There's always catchy, upbeat music and lots of colorful shots. Intensity is created by packing so much visual information into a short time. The cool famous folks make you feel like they're talking straight to you. You feel a one-on-one connection with the star onscreen. The message is that if you just wear this kind of jean or that kind of sneaker, eat one kind of candy bar or drink a certain soda, then your whole life will be as colorful, exciting, intense, and upbeat as theirs.

WHAT'S WRONG WITH THIS PICTURE?

So what if advertising does influence you to buy one brand instead of another? In some cases, there's no problem.

But what if suddenly you really want those designer jeans or expensive running shoes—and you can't afford them? That's exactly what happened when companies started advertising high-priced sneakers by using sports heroes like Bo and Michael. Teens and even younger children were stealing, dealing, and occasionally killing, all in the name of sneakers.

Some teenagers work 20, 30, even 40 hours a week just to buy the latest fashions. They often spend more time working than in school. How else could they afford sneakers that cost more than one hundred dollars?

Companies that advertise certain brands count on people wanting to show off. Brandname products can become status symbols. But did you ever wonder exactly what wearing a status symbol proves? Is it the kind of status you want? Maybe dressing to help save the environment, buying GreenCotton, shopping at thrift stores are the true status symbols for the '90s. Do you want the status of an earth destroyer—or an earth saver?

For example, some jeans are good for the environment now. Levi Strauss is strong on lots of social issues—and Levi sells jeans made of cotton that grows naturally in different colors. Do jeans with a fancier label and a price tag to match fit any better or last any longer? Chances are they show off the designer more than your own good taste. As Najah, a 17-year-old from the Bronx, says, "People go crazy with Benetton and The Gap and Polo and all that garbage just because it has a little sign on it. What's so special about a shirt that says Champion when you could buy a cotton shirt and put your own name on it? "

"It's ridiculous that people pay above the average price for a sweatshirt that advertises a company's name," adds Matthew Paice, 20. "The company should pay the wearer!"

If sales of brandnames are any indication though, Najah and Matthew are unusual. It takes a lot of self-confidence to buy what's best for you and your budget, regardless of the brand. So think about why you choose the products you buy. Do they offer better quality? Better fit? Better style? Better value? A better social record?...or just better commercials?

SMOKE SCREEN

Up to now we've been talking about advertising and fashion. If you want to spend your money on expensive stuff, it might hurt your budget (or your parents' budget!). If you buy from a company that tests on animals, it might hurt the animals. If you buy stuff you don't really need, it might hurt the environment. But one type of advertising, if successful, is a matter of life and death.

Cigarette smoking kills almost half a million Americans every year—and two and a half million people worldwide. Yet tobacco companies like RJR Nabisco and Philip Morris spend $3 billion a year on advertising and promoting cigarettes—and guess who is their prime target? You. That's why cigarette companies advertise cigarettes:

- on billboards and trucks near schools;
- at sports events;
- in movies featuring teenagers smoking;
- on candy cigarettes;
- with free cigarettes at rock concerts;
- in youth-oriented magazines;
- and using cartoon characters.

One of the most famous examples of a company marketing cigarettes to young people is RJR Nabisco's cartoon character Joe Camel. Old Joe, as he is now known, was first introduced five years ago. Today so many kids recognize and like him that many experts think more teenagers are smoking as a direct result. In fact, this ad campaign is apparently so effective for RJR Nabisco that they refuse to stop using Joe—even though the U.S. Surgeon General and the American Medical Association demanded Old Joe go.

How well does this type of cigarette advertising pay off? Consider: adult smoking is decreasing while teenage smoking is on the rise. Kids spend one billion dollars a year on cigarettes. Nicotine is one of the most addictive drugs, so young people, once hooked, tend to keep spending money on cigarettes as they grow up. Pretty smart advertising strategy. Do you buy it?

AD MAD

Is there any way to fight back against billions of dollars of advertising? You bet! Here's how:

- First, look at ads more critically. Try to figure out whether an ad is giving you information you need about a product or just a bunch of pretty pictures and sexy music. Does the ad contain any material that puts down people because of their color, sex, or age? Does the ad make you want a product you may not really need?

- Do the clothes you wear provide free advertisements for companies? They do if you buy jeans, T-shirts, and other items with brandnames plastered all over them. You can either remove those labels or avoid designer clothes.

- Tell your teachers and administrators you object to advertising in school. Speak up in class, and at school board and PTA meetings.

- You could cut down on how much TV you watch. If you don't want to, then consider taping your favorite shows. That way you can fast forward through the commercials—and save time.

- If you order from catalogs or subscribe to magazines, you receive a lot of direct mail, another form of advertising. Let a direct mail association know you don't want any more junk mail. (See page 232 for address.) Bonus points for helping the environment too!

- When you buy something and are asked for your address, tell the salesperson you don't want the information sold or used for marketing purposes. Even grocery stores sometimes give companies information on you and your buying habits.

- Join an organization that studies commercialism, makes recommendations on how to change it, and offers magazines or newsletters with information on ads. (See page 232 for names and addresses.)

- There are two excellent groups dedicated to fighting teen smoking addiction and cigarette advertising aimed at teens: STAT (Stop Teenage Addiction To Tobacco) and Smokefree Educational Services, Inc. They put out newsletters, books, and sponsor a poster contest for kids. (See page 232 for addresses.)

- Write companies or call their toll-free customer service numbers to let them know when you're deciding what to buy, you care more about the environment or minority or women's advancement and less about commercials.

- Rely on **Students Shopping for a Better World** rather than advertisements.

CHAPTER 4

Money Matters

MONEY MATTERS

Now that you're more aware of advertising pressure or environmental concerns, maybe you won't be spending as much. What are you going to do with the cash you've saved? A good place to start is with a financial plan.

Financial planning means setting goals for how you want to spend your money; managing your income and credit; protecting what you own; saving money; and checking your plan regularly to see how it's working. By using a financial plan, you can save up for big items instead of frittering money away on little everyday things. A financial plan might help you get to the college of your choice, ride a great racing bike, or take a fantasy vacation.

It turns out that the majority of high school students don't know enough about checking and savings accounts, food buying, credit, and other subjects to create a financial plan. When the Consumer Federation of America tested 428 teenagers on these consumer issues, they all flunked. Could you answer questions about any of the following topics?

- What type of lender charges the highest interest rates?
- What's the purpose of a credit bureau? What can you do if a credit report about you is wrong?
- How much do car insurance rates differ?
- Should you look at a loan's annual percentage rate or the monthly payment?
- What kind of grocery store usually has the lowest prices?

If you don't know the answers, you're not alone. But there is help available through free financial planning programs for high school students. The programs consist of a series of lesson plans for teachers, student workbooks, and even computer videos.

One of the best financial planning courses is:
High School Financial Planning Program
College For Financial Planning
4695 South Monaco St.
Denver, CO 80237
(303)220-1200

Why not ask a teacher to look into one of these programs? Your wallet might thank you. Meanwhile, here's how to turn a plan that's financially responsible into a plan that's socially responsible, too.

CHECKING IT OUT

Believe it or not, there is such a thing as a socially responsible bank. These banks try to invest their customers' money in companies and ventures that are good for the world as well as for profits.

In the past, loan officers at banks would automatically deny loan applications from certain neighborhoods without even checking on the applicant's credit record. They'd actually mark those poor sections on maps with a red pencil, so the practice was called "redlining." Today, some banks are doing the opposite. Instead of avoiding certain areas, loan officers encourage loans to these neighborhoods, especially those in which the bank is located. This is called "greenlining."

South Shore Bank of Chicago (1-800-669-7725), for example, gives loans to minorities to help build up run-down neighborhoods. Here are a few more greenlining banks:

- Community Capital Bank, Brooklyn (718-802-1212)
- Elk Horn Bank and Trust, Arkansas (501-246-5811)
- Indiana National Bank (1-800-343-4300)
- Vermont National Bank (1-800-367-8862)

Usually these banks will let you open an account by mail and most of them have special no-service charge accounts for people under 18.

If these banks aren't convenient, what else can you do? No matter where you live you can order your checks from a company that donates money to good causes such as Greenpeace, Mothers Against Drunk Driving, and 30 others. Write or call Message! Check Corporation, P.O. Box 3206, Seattle, WA 98114 (800)243-2565.

Beware of banks that say they're specially for kids. Often their terms are not very good for young people. For example, First Children's Bank, which started out in F.A.O. Schwarz toy store in New York and moved to Park Avenue, is open to anyone under 18. You only need $50 to open an account. So far, so good. Now the bad news: unless you keep at least $500 in an account, there is a $10 monthly fee! And the bank does nothing special to benefit children.

But don't let this discourage you. Often smaller savings banks are more user-friendly for teens because they don't have minimum balance requirements. It's worth it to shop around before choosing a bank.

If you just can't find a bank or credit union near you that will let you keep your size account, check out a program called "Save For America." It's in 13 states already, doesn't charge any fees, and even gives you a dollar to start an account! Your school's PTA has to cosponsor Save for America, so you'd need to ask for some help from your parents. Call (206)746-0331 for more information.

Checking and savings accounts are a good idea, no matter how young you are. They inspire you to take more control of your money. Maybe even more important, when it comes time to apply for a credit card or a student loan, you will have developed and proven your financial responsibility by managing your own checking account well. If you have a savings account, you can use it as collateral for credit or loans.

A DIFFERENT APPROACH

There is an alternative to regular banks called credit unions. Credit unions are member-owned, democratically controlled, nonprofit financial cooperatives. A group of people who often have something in common—either work, school, union, or location—join together to form a credit union. Service for members is the main goal, rather than making money for stockholders. The philosophy of credit unions is "people helping people." How do they help? They offer what a bank does, including checking and savings accounts, student loans, and good interest rates.

There are 14,000 credit unions in the U.S. and many offer special programs for student members. In addition, there are 23 high school credit unions and 25 college campus credit unions. For more information, you can write or call the National Credit Union Youth Involvement Board, P.O. Box 391, Madison, WI 53701, (608)238-5851. We've provided a complete list of high school and college credit unions on page 236.

COOL CREDIT CARDS

Did you know that about half of American teenagers use their own or their parents' credit cards? If you switched to a cause-related credit card, you could be helping the environment or saving endangered species or promoting world peace or advancing women and minorities.

Called "affinity" cards, this is how they work: a bank markets its credit card to the members of a nonprofit organization devoted to a good cause. Some examples are Sierra Club, Rainforest Action Network, Amnesty International, Co-op America, Child Welfare League, World Wildlife Fund, and America's Black Colleges. Every time a member uses one of these special credit cards, a small percentage of the charge—or a fixed amount—is donated to the sponsoring organization.

For example, the Working Assets charge card donates to one of 30 different environmental or peace groups 5 cents every time you charge. Cardholders get to vote on how to divide the money.

Co-op America, which links socially responsible businesses and consumers, and prints the Boycott Action News, offers members a VISA card. By using the card, members donate 1/2% of their purchases to Co-op America.

Those credit card charges can really add up to making a difference: in one year, card holders contributed almost half a million dollars to the Sierra Club!

There are more than 1,000 affinity cards in this country. For a list of some to get you started, see page 235.

INVESTING IN A BETTER WORLD

If you want to get really adventurous, you might consider investing in the stock market or a mutual fund or a money market fund. There are socially responsible investment firms that can help you to invest in socially responsible companies. Working Assets, Dreyfus Third Century, and Covenant are a few of the mutual funds that specialize in investing in the best companies they can find.

There are financial research groups that can also help you invest in socially responsible companies. The Council on Economic Priorities has a department called SCREEN that rates many kinds of companies in 11 issue areas: charitable giving, family benefits, workplace issues, minority advancement, women's advancement, disclosure of information, animal testing, involvement in South Africa, community outreach, nuclear and military contracts, and the environment.

The Council on Economic Priorities also has a book called **THE BETTER WORLD INVESTMENT GUIDE** (Prentice-Hall, 1991). It provides information on the social responsibility of 100 companies you might want to invest in and lists other social responsibility investment resources, such as the Social Investment Forum.

CHAPTER 5

Your Job/Your Career

From Fast Food to Fast Track?

YOUR JOB/YOUR CAREER: FROM FAST FOOD TO FAST TRACK

PART-TIME PARADISE?

Have you ever seen old photographs of children, their faces covered with soot, coming out of coal mines? Or standing in factories working dangerous machines? Child labor around the turn of the century was extremely hazardous. Children as young as seven or eight worked long hours under brutal conditions for very little money. For many children, school was nonexistent. If they wanted food and shelter, they had to work. There were no laws to protect them—none until 1938!

Finally that year the government passed the Fair Labor Standards Act, to control child labor in all 50 states. This child labor law helped a lot. So why do we still need child labor laws today? Unfortunately these laws did not end the problem of children suffering because of their jobs. New dangers face today's young workers. Every year approximately 100,000 teenagers are hurt while working. The majority of injuries are in the restaurant industry. In one year alone, 139 teens were killed in the workplace. Just two years ago, the Labor Department found nearly 11,000 child labor violations in a three-day, cross-country search.

Five and a half million people aged 12 to 17 work. Two-thirds of those jobs are at fast-food restaurants, according to one child labor expert. Supermarket and convenience store jobs are the next most common place for teens to work. There also are lots of teenagers working for relatives or in agriculture. Child labor laws do not apply to odd jobs such as babysitting or walking dogs.

Child labor laws are designed to protect young people from job-related injuries. If a 14-year-old loses an arm by operating a dangerous machine the effects are serious and long-reaching. That person will no longer be able to choose among many careers.

The second reason these laws were passed is to make sure that young people have time and energy for their most important job: education. After all, an estimated 95% of teenagers work to have extra spending money, not to help support themselves. So a part-time job should always take a backseat to school work and activities. Child labor laws help protect you from being asked to work hours that may interfere with school.

IT'S THE LAW

There are two kinds of child labor laws. The Fair Labor Standards Act is a federal law that includes the following rules:

- **Children under 14 years old may not be employed EXCEPT by their parents; as actors; or as newspaper deliverers.**
- **14- and 15-year-olds may not work during school hours; before 7 am or after 7 pm (except in the summer); more than three hours a day on school days; more than 18 hours a week during school weeks; more than eight hours a day on nonschool days; more than 40 hours a week during nonschool weeks.**
- **Children under 18 years old may not work in hazardous occupations including explosives manufacturing, motor vehicle driving, mining, logging, meat slaughtering or packing, brick or tile manufacturing, wrecking operations, roofing, excavation, or jobs that expose them to radioactive substances. These minors are also prohibited from operating dangerous machines such as power woodworking machines; power-driven hoisting machines; circular saws, band saws and guillotine shears; metal-forming, punching, and shearing ma-**

chines; bakery machines; paper baling machines; and power-driven slicing and grinding machines.
- **Once you reach 18, child labor laws no longer apply.**

Each state has its own child labor laws too. If there is a difference between the state and the federal laws, the strictest one "wins." Let's say Ben, a 16-year-old who lives in New York, gets a job at McDonald's. The federal law says he can work as many hours as he wants a week. But New York state law says he can work only 28 hours a week during the school year and no later than 10 pm on school nights. Ben and his employer must obey the stricter New York state law.

If you get a part-time job, how can you find out what laws apply to you? It's not always easy. There is no child labor law education process. Many states do require minors to obtain an employment certificate—often called a work permit—before they can get a job. Wherever you apply for your work permit, you can ask for information. But often the person who does the paperwork isn't up to date with the law. The best approach is to call your state Department of Labor office. We listed all the phone numbers for you on page 239.

Finding out which companies have violated child labor laws is very difficult and time-consuming. You can ask the Department of Labor but you have to know the exact name and address of the owner of the business. For example, if CEP wanted to know about Burger Kings across the country, we would have had to have the exact addresses and names of each of Burger King's 5,349 franchises! But you can find out about a company's specific location by writing to your state's Department of Labor. The information they give you will be a good clue as to whether you need to be concerned about possible exploitation.

AFTER THE INTERVIEW

Once you actually have a job offer, it's a good idea to discuss any special conditions with your supervisor—BEFORE you start work. That way you can feel out how aware your boss is of safe and age-appropriate work. You may also want to know how flexible your boss is going to be—above and beyond what's required by law. You can say something like, "Sometimes I have to take my mother to the doctor because she has arthritis. So although I'm signed up for Tuesdays and Fridays, sometimes her appointments will be those days. Will that be okay?" Or, "I'm almost flunking French. When it comes time for the French final, I've got to spend more time with French and less with you. All right?"

The response you get at this point is a way to tell your employer's attitude. If they are not willing to work with your French final or your mother's arthritis, consider not taking the job. Think about what is most important to you. Is it buying your next pair of Reeboks? Or is it your family, your education—your future?

Of course, the right job can be invaluable. A job should help you learn something positive, provide references for college applications or after college work, or, at the least, help you save for college or basic expenses. Often a summer internship or volunteer work offers you more than making minimum wage at McDonald's.

STAY ALERT, STAY ALIVE

Three machines often used in the places teens are most likely to work should be a red flag. Not only are these machines illegal to operate until you're 18, they are very dangerous. Watch out for these machines. If your boss asks you to use one, it's a serious violation of child labor laws for obvious safety reasons.

1. **POWER-DRIVEN SLICING MACHINES** in delis, supermarkets, or fast-food restaurants—anywhere they slice meats, cheeses, or vegetables. Minors are prohibited from operating, setting up, adjusting, cleaning, oiling, or repairing these machines.
2. **PAPER BALERS,** large electric-powered machines in bins where you throw supermarket or fast-food supply cartons. The baler squashes the paper and ties it up. It's illegal for anyone under 18 even to throw things into it.
3. **INDUSTRIAL DOUGH MIXERS,** huge vats with big metal blades, found in Dominos, Dunkin Donuts, Pizza Hut, and other big chains where kids work.

TIME AND MONEY

Although these are the most dangerous violations, they aren't the most likely ones you'll find yourself up against. The laws on hours are much more commonly found broken or ignored—maybe because hours abuse is the easiest to find. All labor officials have to do is check time cards—or show up at 10 pm. Late night hours or too many hours per day are the most common violation.

Another way young people get zapped in the workplace is with wages. If you just got your very first job, you may be thrilled by making any amount. But the law says your employer must pay you the minimum wage—so be sure you know what that amount is and don't be afraid to ask for it! Internships are special work arrangements and don't fall under minimum wage guidelines.

If you're asked to work "off the books"—to be paid in cash—watch out. That's usually a good sign your boss is employing you illegally. What should you do if that happens to you—or you are asked to work more hours than you know is okay or to operate an illegal machine?

HOW TO HANDLE A PROBLEM

Before you do anything, remember that you have certain rights as a worker in general and as a child worker specifically. Lots of times teenagers are too intimidated to ask questions at work or to say no to an inappropriate request. Employers know this and sometimes take advantage of it. Don't let that happen to you.

When you have a concern about your job, go first to your immediate supervisor. This may be someone called the sandwich captain or the assistant manager. You'd say—politely—"Remember last week I mentioned I have exams. Could you please let me know whether we can change my hours?" Or: "I worked really late last week. I'd like to get off at a more reasonable time."

If you do not get a satisfactory response, try the manager or whoever is the next in the chain of command. If you don't know, ask if there's anyone else you can talk to—maybe it's someone called a regional human resource manager. The titles vary. The point is to keep trying within the organization.

If you still get nowhere and you believe child labor law is being violated, then call your state Department of Labor. Explain what you think the problem is, that you've already tried communicating with your supervisor, and ask what to do next. And don't forget, if you feel too tongue-tied or shy, you can always ask your parents to make the call for you.

LIFE AFTER SCHOOL

Do you remember when you were little how often you were asked "What do you want to be when you grow up?"

But did anyone ever ask "How do you want to live? What are your values? How will you make a living and keep your self-respect? What will you give back to the world when you've been given so much?"

If you want to be socially responsible when you "grow up," you need to start thinking about these kinds of questions while you're still a student. What exactly is a socially responsible career? There are lots of ways to look at it. One college workshop came up with the following definitions:

- respect for global vision
- support for co-workers and clients
- commitment to being in a non-exploitative environment
- promoting health
- being responsible for one's actions
- not contributing to war or the military
- commitment to equal opportunities for all.

Since students at Humboldt State University began the Graduation Pledge Alliance in 1987, students at more than 70 high schools and colleges have signed the Graduation Pledge of Social and Environmental Responsibility at graduation ceremonies each year. It reads: "I ______________________ pledge to investigate thoroughly and take into account the social and environmental consequences of any job opportunity I consider." For more information on the Graduation Pledge Alliance, write PO Box 4439, Arcata, CA 95521.

THE RIGHT JOB

There are three main ways to choose a socially responsible career.

The first route is to pick a field that is, by definition, socially responsible. You'd develop useful skills in a certain area such as the environment and then find a job in that area. Of course some jobs with "environment" in their titles are to protect and defend a corporation's bad environmental practices. Other traditionally socially responsible fields include social work, medicine, human rights, and teaching. If you choose this path, there are more and more colleges and universities that offer special majors like environmental studies and graduate programs like global resource management. But a word of caution: Schools can gift wrap themselves through "green" marketing programs that offer more tinsel than substance. Students can often do a better job of preparing for an environmental career by majoring in hard science or finding a good internship with a dual major. College consumers need to tread as carefully as any kind of consumer.

THE RIGHT ORGANIZATION

The second way is to choose the right organization. Although public sector jobs tend to pay less, they're harder to get. So you can try the "foot in the door" approach with a group that you feel is doing socially responsible work. For example, you could get a secretarial job or internship and try to work your way up at Amnesty International, Greenpeace, the NAACP, the Sierra Club—any organization you support. (Lots of the staff here at Council on Economic Priorities started out as student interns!) Often, such organizations are either nonprofit or government agencies.

Jobs at public interest organizations offer good learning experiences and may give greater responsibility sooner. If you choose this path, be sure your values don't blind you to the nature of the job itself, however. You need to really be committed to a cause to put up with the tedious tasks in certain entry-level positions.

Many resources are available to help you find jobs with socially responsible organizations. One is Public Allies: The National Center for Careers in Public Life at (202)232-6800. Another is ACCESS, which publishes a newsletter that lists jobs and internships with nonprofit groups: Community Jobs, 50 Beacon St., Boston, MA 02108. More of these kinds of publications are listed in Chapter Eleven on page 231.

THE RIGHT STUFF

A third path to social responsibility is to get a traditional corporate job with the "best" company you can find—and then keep working to help that company improve its own track record in the areas that are important to you.

For example, you might want to be a lawyer, accountant, administrator, or manager in a large corporation. But you don't want to work for a company that pollutes rivers, dumps chemicals, or discriminates against women or minorities.

Can you have your corporate cake and eat it too? Yes, according to career counselor Skip Sturman. "You can find shining stars of social responsibility in almost any field. A lot depends not just on the setting itself but on the mindset people bring to their work. Increasing numbers of businesses rate very high on a number of social scales."

On the practical side, there isn't much time to research a company once a job offer is made. They want you to respond as soon as possible. It's better to try and find out all you can about a company you're interested in before your job interview. Career counselors tell you to do that anyway as part of your preparation, so you ask intelligent questions and impress the interviewer. The more you know, the more you can ask about whether the company's values are in harmony with your own. Here are some issues that deal with social responsibility:

- whether the company is involved with military contracting, nuclear weapons, animal testing for non-medical products
- environment (overpackaging, polluting, energy use, product)

- community (openness, accountability, contributions)
- employee relations (wages and benefits, working conditions, unions, security)
- race and gender (discrimination, affirmative action, sexual harassment, pay differential, minority vendor programs)

You should be able to answer most of those questions by doing your own research. You can check books such as this one; use sources like newspaper and magazine articles, annual reports, and computer databases; talk to people who work at the company or who used to work there; check with watchdog organizations such as Sierra Club, Corporate Crime Reporter, Interfaith Center for Corporate Responsibility, and, last but not least, the Council on Economic Priorities.

If, before the interview, you uncover anything about the company that you cannot accept, you're better off not interviewing with that organization in the first place. You don't want to go so far as a job interview at a company only to find yourself saying "Gee, your whole business is based on weaponry, which I totally oppose." Make your first cuts before applying for a job, and then use the interview to make sure your good feelings about a company hold up.

IN THE DOOR

Once at the interview, you don't want to attack the interviewer by asking "Does your company harm the environment or oppress anyone?" Avoid putting the interviewer on the defensive. But it is fair to ask questions based on information you've already gleaned. Say you noticed in the annual report the organization says it favors voluntarism. You could ask them to elaborate on how they encourage employees to give back to their communities. Or, if you have not read anything about a volunteer program, you could ask whether or not this is something the company emphasizes. Try to ask questions that give interviewers an opening but do not box them into a corner.

Another good example of a general question you could safely ask in an interview is: "I've been reading a lot about a dual bottom line, corporations caring not only about profit but also about giving back to the community. Would you say a dual bottom line reflects your corporation's mission?" The answer to this question should give you an overview of how the company relates to the idea of social responsibility.

CHAPTER 6

Social Action

Have You Got What it Takes?

SOCIAL ACTION: HAVE YOU GOT WHAT IT TAKES?

If you've read this far, maybe you feel as if you'd like to do more to help the world. To look beyond your home, see a problem, and try to do something about it—that's social action. Maybe you're not quite sure what one teenager could accomplish. Here are real-life examples of five young people who have made a difference—before they even graduated from high school.

IN THEIR OWN WORDS

Environmentalism

Jennifer Rubenstein, from Pittsford, New York, is a 17-year-old senior at The Harley School.

I used to think that no one had the power to change the world, except the president or James Bond. I read about air and water pollution, decreasing biodiversity, and the hole in the ozone layer, but I took no action because I didn't think I could make a difference. My frustration grew as I saw that, despite what they said, our government and the large corporations that were doing a lot of the polluting were more interested in short-term economic profit than they were in environmental integrity and long-term economic gain.

So what could I do? I was a measly little freshman, too scared to walk by the seniors at my school, much less do anything to help save the world. I was just about to give up on the whole idea, when I heard about a club some students at my school had started called Global Awareness Project. I went to a meeting, and immediately realized that there were many things I could do to help make the world a better place.

That was four years ago. I am now a senior, and the president of the Global Awareness Project (GAP). This year we helped run the recycling program at my school, sponsored "Energy Days," started composting our school's cafeteria waste, and presented four assemblies, including a biodiversity day. We held an Endangered Species Day: most students were an endangered species and people in my group were "causes." Every 15 minutes someone was made "extinct" with a big red sticker. At the end of the day, we had a funeral service, where we talked about causes and played the funeral march.

GAP also gives kids at my school the chance to volunteer at soup kitchens, community farms, and other places. We had a Buy a Leaf, Get a Cookie sale. We had everyone buy and decorate a leaf and put it up on a tree. Then we gave 10% of the profits to the Nature Conservancy.

We sponsored a letter-writing party to write letters to our congresspeople on various issues.

I co-chaired a Rochester area High School Youth Ending Hunger Conference for 75 kids from 18 schools. We offered skills workshops, brainstorming, and project groups. The keynote speaker was the former president of World Bank.

I've given numerous talks about hunger to local youth groups and at other schools. I co-hosted the North American Regional Meeting of the Global Youth Conference, a five-day conference on hunger in Washington, D.C. for 250 students.

Working on these projects has brought me to a few conclusions. First, I realized that we are all responsible for what happens to our world. It's easy to sit back and blame our government or the large corporations. It's harder to remember that we voted them into office, and we buy the products they sell us. If you oppose Dow Chemical Company polluting the environment, don't buy Dow products. If you want government leaders to pass stronger clean air legislation, write them a letter, then walk to your friends' houses instead of taking the car.

The idea is, use public pressure to help make change for the better, but live your personal life in a way that's consistent with your vision. Which brings me to my next point...

The absolute worst, most horrible, miserable thing anybody can possibly say when it comes to the environment is "but I'm only one small person, I can't make a difference." If I could tell you anything, drill anything into your brain so hard that you would never forget it, here is what it would be: you can make a difference. You, sitting there, whoever you are reading this, can get up off your butt right now and do something that will help make this world a nicer place. Write a letter, clean a park, hug your mother. You have everything you need to start, and nothing in the world to lose.

If, along the way, you begin to feel that it's hopeless, or a lost cause, take a short break. Visit a friend, go for a walk in the woods, play with your baby brother, and remember what Henry David Thoreau said:
"....If one advances confidently in the direction of his dreams, and endeavors to live the life which he has imagined, he will meet with a success unexpected in common hours..."

Environmentalism

Louisa Michaels is 13 and lives in Kensington, California.

When I was nominated for school president in sixth grade, I made a speech about how much garbage the school produced and how a lot of it could be recycled. I began telling kids why recycling is important.

I told them that, first, the world is everyone's environment, including the animals and future generations. Everything is part of the environment. Everyone should care for it.

I said recycling is so simple and in the long run if we don't do it, this is what we'll see through future windows: landfill in your backyard, garbage everywhere, a city living on old newspapers and cans, and no trees or birds anywhere. This picture was scary so I got 580 out of 600 kids to sign a recycling petition. We had recycling monitors who made sure trash got sorted into the correct bins: cans, plastic lunch trays, bags, or box drinks.

When I got to middle school, I advised student council to start recycling bins for different recyclable kinds of trash—and to my surprise they did! I also wrote to magazines that did articles on saving the earth but didn't even print on recycled paper. How could they tell us to be earth conscious when they weren't doing so themselves? Didn't they want a good environment for themselves, their kids, and their pets?

My idea for a clean world includes local recycling centers, saving the rainforests, and helping the animals that have lost tree homes to trees that have been cut down. Everybody needs to take part! Many good things can come out of caring for the environment, such as unity, a cleaner earth, even learning to care for each other.

You may not be able to vote yet, but don't be afraid to speak your mind, especially to adults. I've found that if I do this, adults who usually don't vote will start to vote or they'll feel guilty because here you are, not even grown up, and already speaking your mind about important issues. Maybe then adults will think about making life easier for us kids in the future by voting for propositions like those that help save the rainforests.

It's easy to make suggestions about recycling to your student council or city hall. Even if they won't listen, at least you know that you've taken your first step to saving the earth. Keep trying!

Minority Advancement

Eric Boone, an 18-year-old sophomore from Hempstead, Long Island, attends Wake Forest University in North Carolina.

A homeless man moans as he feels the pain of his hunger. A baby born to a crack-addicted mother cries as she lies in an incubator. A mother screams as she falls on the casket of her slain 16-year-old son. These are the cries of black America, cries that have fallen on the deaf ears of politicians and bureaucrats. These cries ring in my head and cause me a pain that I mean to relieve. They desperately call for solutions and I do my best to offer assistance. I rise so quickly to the challenge, I can still feel the blood rushing to my head.

My rise as a civil rights activist and leader began at my first meeting of the Hempstead Youth Council of the National Association for the Advancement of Colored People. As I witnessed the organization's activity, vitality, and efficiency, I was captivated and immediately joined. It was there I received my training, a new level of awareness, and a new commitment to the struggle. I couldn't have anticipated what was to follow or how I was to come to lead.

Within a few months of my membership, I ran for youth council president. To my surprise, I won by a unanimous vote and attended the NAACP's National Convention in Los Angeles. The convention introduced me to thousands of black young people we don't hear of in the media. They are the ones reaching for the highest goals. They are committed to the betterment of the African-American community. They filled me with a sense of pride and issued a call to me that I could no longer deny.

Although I was a new member, I was highlighted as a youth leader and featured as a panelist in a national workshop on education. The Los Angeles Times included me in an article on the convention.

When I came back to New York, I was fired up and ready to go. We held voter registration campaigns, Kwanzaa celebrations, a business basics program, conducted sexual awareness programs, held an Afro-centric fashion show, and featured speakers throughout the year. We sponsored workshops on

"Developing Positive Self-Images and Discipline in Black Children" with the hope of lowering the dropout rate at a local high school. We won awards on a state, regional, and national level. I won the 1991 Gloster B. Current national youth leadership award. The best was yet to come.

At the next annual convention in Houston, Texas, I was elected to the National Youth Work Committee of the NAACP and served as its chairman and director ex-officio on the National Board of Directors. At 17 years old, I went from running a local youth council to representing the national Youth and College Division, 50,000 members strong. Now in my second term, my role is to serve youth, voice their concerns, and address the issues of importance to them.

In the past two years, I have flown to Washington, D.C. to vote with the NAACP board on Clarence Thomas' Supreme Court nomination. I have traveled around the country giving speeches, conducting workshops on leadership training and voter education. I am currently serving on the 21-member search committee for our next executive director, an official who is, by title alone, one of the most influential black Americans. I've also reactivated the college chapter of Wake Forest University and serve as its vice president.

Often when I tell people of my activities, they ask how I have done so much at such an early age. The question should be more appropriately: how could I not do as much? The community I am working to improve is the community that I will inherit. My conscience will not allow me to sit on the side lines. It calls for me to answer the cries of black America that for so long have been denied. It calls for me to rise. If people before me could take beatings, be hosed down, bitten by dogs, and jailed, I can handle blood rushing to my head as I rise....

Lillian Potter, 16, is a junior at Whitman High School in Bethesda, Maryland.

On the third day of my freshman year I was in a history class when a friend asked our teacher how long the essays we were writing should be. My teacher asked me to stand, and pointing to my skirt, he said, "Your papers should be just like Lillian's skirt—long enough to cover the subject yet short enough to be interesting."

I decided I needed to do something. There were a lot of girls at Whitman who were being intimidated and treated unfairly. We needed a voice. So my friend Liz and I contacted our county NOW (National Organization for Women) chapter, and they offered to sponsor. Liz and I set up an advisory board consisting of a vice-principal, our NOW faculty sponsor, my father, and a representative from the county NOW chapter.

We had a booth at an all-school open house, distributed flyers, held round-table discussions, and made announcements about our new club.

We organized a date rape seminar for all seniors and next year hope to expand it for all four grades. During Women's History Month, we held student facilitated discussions on sexual harassment and the role of the modern woman, had poetry readings, and arranged art displays.

I have spoken on behalf of Whitman NOW at several educational equity forums in the county. I sat on a NOW panel with politicians, parents, and health care providers to debate teen access to abortion. I have given speeches on abortion rights and birth control.

Much of my time is spent organizing—getting groups of students to work at a battered women's shelter, demonstrate, train as clinic defenders, crowd into hearings and legislator's offices. We also do a lot of grassroots work like phone banks, fundraising, and envelope stuffing.

One of our biggest challenges stemmed from complaints we received from female athletes. Apparently the cheerleaders cheered only at the boys' games—not the girls! A little research showed that the county required cheerleaders to spend 105 1/2 hours annually at boys' sports, 56 at coed sports, and 33 1/2 at girls' sports. Obviously, girls were shortchanged, in direct violation of Title IX, the federal law that says men and women are equal in their educational opportunities.

Our administrators were unwilling to change our adherence to the county rule. The athletic director said that the cheerleaders were needed for "crowd control" since there were larger crowds at the boys' games. He and the cheerleader sponsor alluded to what they called our lack of femininity and school spirit. The athletic director laughed at me until I'd end up crying.

It was very difficult. People I didn't even know would shout at me or give me dirty looks. Even some of my friends stayed away.

Then I met the girls' basketball coach. We made plans to confront and change the problems in the athletic department as well as the administration's treatment of girls.

This battle has just finished its third year and is still not resolved. We plan to file formal Title IX charges with the Equal Employment Opportunity Commission. I doubt it will be resolved by the time I graduate in another year.

There still are amazing inequities for men and women in our society. If everyone just sits back and comments, nothing will ever get done. When I feel tired and despondent, all I have to do is look at the Anita Hill–Clarence Thomas hearings. If you are not an optimist, if you don't honestly believe that all the blood, sweat and tears will pay off, then you can never change things. We have no time for apathy or cynicism. We have a lot to do.

I will fight and persevere and win.

Animal Welfare

David Berman is a 17-year-old junior at Lower Merion High School in Merion, Pennsylvania.

In 9th grade I took a course on advanced animal rights through the American Anti-Vivisection Society. When the course ended, several of the students and I felt we could not let all the things we had learned go to waste—we had to take action. That is how Students Protecting Animal Rights and the Environment (SPARE) came about. I have been president since our founding.

We have been committed to student activism. Our goal is to educate our peers about various animal rights and environmental issues. We want to mobilize the youth of today in order to alleviate animal suffering and environmental destruction and to show that students care about their world. We are totally student run and organized. We sponsor many events throughout the year, including protests, tabling, fundraising, letter writing, boycotting campaigns—and even vegetarian potluck dinners.

Our events are mainly in the Philadelphia area, but we have members from several states representing dozens of schools. We have held meetings with invited speakers at the Free Library in Philadelphia. We encourage students to sponsor events in their areas and to start local SPARE chapters. We inform students of events sponsored by larger organizations in the hope they'll participate. We also provide free literature on a number of issues from our office (a room in my house) to any interested student.

I have been president of the animal rights club at my school, Students for the Ethical Treatment of Animals (SETA), for two years. We do as much as we can within the confines of school. Our main purpose is to educate the student body on animal issues. We hold weekly meetings, and make many posters which we hang in the hallways. We have had showcases, invited speakers, and organized a fur protest. I run all the meetings and try to bring up issues such as pet overpopulation, cosmetic testing, fur, and factory farming.

I have attended more than 20 protests on vivisection, factory farming, carriage horses, hunting, and fur as well as recycling, abortion rights, and peace. As a SPARE member, I have organized my own protests, drawing large crowds of students. I recently spoke at a Fur-Free Philly protest, along with other prominent animal rights activists, and at a conference to teach activists and teachers how to teach animal issues to high school students.

All this effort has resulted in press coverage in the Philadelphia Inquirer, Philadelphia Daily News, Humane Society Newsletter, Anti-Vivisection Magazine, Vegetarian Times, Animals' Agenda, and Animals Voice.

I encourage students to fight not only for animal rights and the environment, but for all positive social change. Animal rights is part of the women's rights, gay rights, and civil rights movements, for we all fight against a form of prejudice. Anyone can make a difference. You don't have to start an entire organization as I did. (Let me tell you that it takes a lot of work!) You can stop eating meat. You can stop buying from companies that remain in the dark ages and test products on animals or pollute our planet. You can write letters, contact your legislators...but you can't leave the problems that exist for someone else to take care of. You have to take action yourself. Hear the animals screaming in the laboratories and factory farms, see our trees being chopped down, and do something about it. Good intentions are not enough.

ARE YOU READY?

It takes a lot of time and energy to make a difference in the world. What Jennifer, David, Lillian, Eric, and Louisa have in common is a strong commitment to an issue.

Before you take social action, think about all the issues. Which one do you feel the most passion for? Have you had any personal experiences in a particular area? What do you think is the most important problem we face today? Is there a specific situation right in your neighborhood you might be able to do something about? Sometimes tackling a small problem and finding a solution is more satisfying than trying to take on the whole world right away. Once you've narrowed it down a little, you're ready to plunge in.

Here are some things you can do. (Information on any publication or group mentioned below is listed in Chapter Eleven.)

- Read *The Kid's Guide to Social Action: How to Solve the Social Problems You Choose—And Turn Creative Thinking Into Positive Action.* This is a terrific book that really goes into detail with lots of concrete examples.
- Start a new club at your school to focus on the issue you pick. This is what David did.
- Contact a national organization you're interested in to see whether you can start a youth chapter in your area. This is what Lillian did.
- Write letters about your concerns to those in charge: legislators, mayors, Congress and Senate members, governors—even the president! Don't forget the heads of corporations.
- Write press releases about your activities to newspapers, radio, and television stations. Check out the *Student Action Guide* for good examples of effective press releases.

- Organize, organize, organize! Find others who believe what you believe, then join forces to propose, research, educate, boycott, petition, protest, lobby—whatever it takes to make changes.
- Advertise your cause—put up posters, make speeches, fundraise to place ads in magazines or newspapers.

GET SET, GO!

Teen adviser Jennifer Rubenstein explains how to start recycling at your school:

Recycling conserves energy, preserves natural resources, and saves room in landfills. It's also an easy, fun way to raise environmental awareness. Here is a list of steps you can take to begin recycling at your school. Before you begin, check the recycling laws that apply to your area to see what, if anything, your school will be **required** to recycle in the near future.

First, call a local recycling center to see what it will accept and how the recyclables must be packaged, bundled, or otherwise treated.

Estimate how much material you're going to have, then decide how you're going to transport it to the recycling center. Will someone from the center pick it up? Will a teacher or local business help?

Present your idea to your principal or school board. It isn't likely that either will reject the project, but you'll increase your chances if you offer a coherent plan. Be sure to mention how **educational** it will be for students to be involved in recycling. Also, try to find an adult adviser for your club. He or she may be able to point out questions you haven't addressed or help you communicate with other adults.

Decide who will collect and package the recyclable material. Arrange for different classes or homerooms to take turns every week. Make sure everyone knows when it's their turn and exactly what they're supposed to do.

Put collection bins in every classroom or hallway, preferably near the wastebaskets. Label separate bins for paper, cans, etc. Try to get a local business or garbage disposal service to donate the bins.

Educate the students at your school. This is the most important part of your project. Make sure everyone knows not only what they have to do, but why they're doing it. Perform skits, hold assemblies, and anything else you can think of to tell people about the importance of recycling and the new recycling program at your school. Posters work well, but remember...you're trying to save paper!

Once you have your basic recycling routine down, go crazy! Find out what's being thrown away in the cafeteria, the administrative office, and other areas. If your school already has a recycling program, this is where you can get creative. Remember, reducing and reusing are a thousand times better than recycling. Can the art department use old milk cartons? Can the elementary school use art department scraps? Can your school begin composting?

Projects like recycling clubs are very challenging, and it's almost guaranteed that along the way you'll run into problems you haven't foreseen. But whatever happens, DON'T GIVE UP! The rewards for you, your school, and the rest of the world are definitely worth your struggle.

CHAPTER 7

How to Use This Guide

HOW TO USE THIS GUIDE

The three chapters that rate companies are each organized differently.

Chapter Eight: Shopping for Your Future: Ratings by Company—Highest and lowest rated companies. Alphabetical list of all the "parent" companies that are in the book. We call them parent companies because they may own subsidiaries or divisions. Listed under each parent company are its brandnames and/or subsidiaries for every product category in the book. Pepsico Inc. is a parent company, for example. Its subsidiaries are Kentucky Fried Chicken, Pizza Hut, and Taco Bell. Its brandnames include Pepsi and Diet Pepsi. Here's where you'll find the company's address and name of the chief executive officer for letter-writing.

Chapter Nine: Shopping for Your Future: Ratings by Product—Arranged by type of product (FAST FOOD, SNACKS, SPORTING GOODS, etc.). Within each of the 18 product categories are parent companies, again listed alphabetically. Under each parent company only the brandnames for that product category are listed; company ratings; and EXTRAS.

Chapter Ten: Shopping for Your Future: Top Teen Brands—Ratings and descriptions of companies that make the brands teenagers buy most, including Nike, Reebok, Levi Strauss, The Gap, Burger King, McDonald's, Pepsi, Coca Cola, Time Warner, Sony, and Procter & Gamble (shampoos like Pert, Prell, Ivory, Head and Shoulders, Pantene, and Vidal Sassoon). Here you will find information that either expands on the ratings or didn't fall into our ratings categories.

Each company is rated on the following issues:
- **Environment**
- **Minority Advancement**
- **Women's Advancement**
- **Disclosure of Information**

These four issues are rated with letter grades:

A = outstanding performance
C = moderate or mixed performance
F = poor performance
I = means incomplete—although we tried very hard, we could not find enough information to assign a rating.

You can use the guide many different ways. Let's say you're in the market for a new pair of sneakers. You could go right to the SNEAKERS/SHOES category in Chapter Nine to find the sneaker company with the best "track" record in whatever area you care most about.

Or maybe you notice that one company has a low environment rating. You'd like to avoid buying anything that company makes. So you turn to Chapter Eight, find the company and check out all its products or subsidiaries.

Finally, you will want to look up ratings for companies that make things you already buy. If you use Crest toothpaste, for example, you might not know what company makes it. But you can go right to the brandname index at the back of the book, look up "Crest," and turn to the page number listed next to it. You'll find Crest on that page under its parent company, Procter & Gamble, in the Dental Care category. You can look at the ratings and Extras—and decide if you want to keep brushing with Crest!

MAKING THE GRADE

How do we decide what grade a company gets? For each issue area, there is a different set of standards. Also, the standards differ slightly depending on what industry the company falls into and how many employees it has. In other words, we would look at a paper company differently from a fast-food company, and a small company differently than a large company.

The grades in this guide are based on information current as of August 1992 and earlier (within the last five years). The information comes from the companies themselves; public documents available at government agencies, libraries and specialized centers, or from citizens groups; and advisers who are experts in our categories. Readers of our previous shopping guides should be aware that the way we assigned ratings for this book differs slightly from past years.

ENVIRONMENT

A=Strong company-wide programs, such as a company-wide environmental policy, alternative energy sources, waste reduction through source reduction, recycling and reuse, non-hazardous manufacturing materials, minimal or no toxic releases, care for natural resources. A record clear of accidents and major violations of environmental regulations.

C=A mixed record or only moderate effort. Some positive programs such as recycling, alternative energy sources and waste reduction. Some problems such as accidents, regulatory infractions, fines, or complaints.

F=A poor record of major violations, accidents and/or lobbying against environmental policies. Minimal or no energy conservation. No effort to minimize its environmental impact and deal with problems it may have created.

I=Not enough information for a grade.

There are many examples of corporations' "green" activities. Procter & Gamble has increased the recycled content of many of its packages. Wal-Mart asked its suppliers for products they claim are better for the environment, and the store highlights these with shelf displays and explanations. Even clothing manufacturers like Levi are trying to come up with "greener" fabrics. On the other hand, Chevron's People Do campaign makes you believe the company is environmentally responsible—yet it has more than $1.5 million in Clean Water Act violation fines.

Some companies advertise products as good for the environment that are not. For example, companies claim you can recycle juice boxes. But very few recycling centers accept juice boxes. How can you tell whether a product is really green? Many groups and individuals are working to answer that question. The federal government issued national guidelines recently which developed standards for environmental terms like recyclable or degradable. Several groups have organized to certify rainforest woods logged in a sustainable manner. The Northeast states have written laws to help reduce toxic chemicals in packaging. Researchers are comparing the environmental impacts of different types of packaging.

Green Seal, a nongovernment eco-labeling program, gives environmentally-friendly products its seal of approval. To carry a Green Seal, a company must be carefully screened by the Green Seal staff.

While many changes still need to be made, it is clear that companies and the government are responding to consumer pressure about environmental issues. In Chapter Two you'll find a long list of things you can do individually to help.

MINORITIES

A=At least three minorities on the board of directors or among top officers (corporate officer level or higher at corporate headquarters or president/chief executive officer of a subsidiary or division).

C=Two minorities on the board or among top officers.

F=One or no minorities on the board or among top officers.

I=Not enough information for a grade.

The Council on Economic Priorities uses the Equal Employment Opportunity Commission's definition of minority, which includes blacks, Native Americans, Hispanics, and Asians. Ratings are also based on Equal Employment Opportunity Commission reports on percentages of minorities among officials and managers; purchasing from minority-owned firms; banking with minority-owned banks; representation of minorities among the company's top 25 salaried employees; programs to encourage the advancement of minorities within the company; and discrimination suits. Ratings are adjusted for company size and industry.

WOMEN

A=At least four women on the board of directors or among top officers (corporate officer level or higher at corporate headquarters or president/chief executive officer of a subsidiary or division).

C=Two or three women on the board or among top officers.

F=Only one or no women on the board or among top officers.

I=Not enough information for a grade.

Ratings are also based on Equal Employment Opportunity Commission reports on percentages of women among officials and managers; purchasing from women-owned firms; representation of women among the company's top 25 salaried employees; programs that encourage the advancement of women within the company; and any discrimination suits. Ratings are adjusted for company size and industry.

The U.S. Department of Labor estimates that three-fourths of all new workers in the 1990s will be minorities or women. But just look at what minorities and women earn compared to white males, according to 1992 Bureau of Labor Statistics:

Black Americans earned $362 per week.
Hispanic Americans earned $323 per week.
White Americans earned $465 per week.
Women working full-time earn only 72 cents for every $1 a man earns.

We've seen a definite pattern in the last few years: slow but steady movement from a token woman to two or maybe three women at the top in many large corporations. But many boards of directors of major companies, like Reebok, still do not have even one female member; even fewer have members of minority groups. American Home Products, which makes Wheatena and Maypo cereals, has no minorities on its board.

Some companies, such as Avon and General Mills, have gone a long way toward the advancement of qualified women and minorities. They use Upward Mobility Committees and minority employee support networks. They advertise in women's and minorities' publications and/or review their personnel managers' records in hiring women and minorities.

In 1991, at least one woman was on the board of directors at 519 of the leading companies. Of the 519 companies, 133 have more than one woman director. Minorities had less representation. It is possible for corporations to support equal employment opportunity even if minorities make up only a small part of the surrounding population or if the company is in an industry where the pool of qualified women is limited. Some companies, such as Nike and Tom's of Maine, have appointed minorities from other geographic areas to their boards—Tom's of Maine was the first company to appoint a Native American.

Companies may choose to keep funds in banks owned by minorities or women, or in banks like South Shore Bank of Chicago, which has turned its entire neighborhood around by making local home mortgage and small business loans available to minorities.

Companies can also try to find suppliers among businesses owned by minorities or women. PepsiCo, for example, has a $240 million minority purchasing program. The growth of minority purchasing and banking programs has been encouraging. In 1972, purchasing programs reported $86 million in business. The National Minority Suppliers Development Council says that by 1990, purchasing programs it monitors exceeded $15 billion.

You may not yet be in the working world. But you can still help support equal opportunity for everyone by supporting companies in this book that receive an A for women's and minority advancement.

DISCLOSURE

A=Company provides ample, up-to-date, useful material on its social programs either by completing CEP's questionnaire or by providing similar information in writing, phone interviews, or publications.

C=Company provides some information either by completing part of CEP's questionnaire or by providing similar information in writing, phone interviews, or publications. Certain key questions left unanswered.

F=Company provides only the most basic information: an annual report, proxy statement and 10K with little social performance information, or less. Or only provides information that is not detailed enough to measure the company's performance.

A company's willingness to share information on its basic operations and its social programs is not only important, it is a sign of good corporate citizenship. Until recently, most corporations have not wanted to provide useful data on social programs—many still fight it. Attempts to require companies to do so by law have been largely unsuccessful.

Though most firms still do not publish information on social performance, many companies with a definite commitment to social responsibility have made it a priority. More and more companies are adding a small section to their annual report describing their commitment. Other companies publish longer reports. Many of these reports are full of feel-good pictures and words but don't really describe the company's social programs. Others routinely inform the public of the social impact of their operations in concrete terms and use a format comparable year to year and among companies. The best ones, such as Bristol-Myers Squibb Co.'s and Ben and Jerry's, document company efforts, demonstrate results or include shortcomings, and use comparable data.

Of the 166 companies rated in this book, only 75 cooperated fully by providing extensive information, 16 provided more limited information, and 75 gave us little or no information. In general, privately held companies were much less willing to cooperate with CEP than a publicly traded company.

EXTRAS

Under the ratings chart is a section called EXTRAS. EXTRAS are just that: extra information about the social impact of a company not reflected in a rating. Some EXTRAS are positive, some are negative, and some are neutral.

Animal Testing. Many individuals and organizations have become concerned with corporations that use animals in their research. Efforts to end the use of animals in testing on consumer products have been successful at many large cosmetics companies such as Revlon and Avon. But other companies that also do not make medical products continue to test on animals. Pain is often inflicted on animals to develop frivolous vanity products.

Roughly 20 million animals are used in lab research each year. The majority are rats and mice; some are dogs, cats and rabbits. Testing by consumer products companies accounts for a tiny fraction of all research animals; the majority are used by drug companies and in government, academic, and medical research—often resulting in lifesaving medical advances.

Animals will continue to be used until we find good alternatives. So we need to make sure that they are used only for good reasons and in cases where no effective alternative to their use has been found. Meanwhile, we must make sure that such uses are as humane as possible.

Some companies, such as Tom's of Maine and The Body Shop, were established with the principle of no animal testing. Other companies, such as Colgate Palmolive and Procter & Gamble, have substantially reduced the number of animals used and/or actively joined the search for alternative test methods.

Animal rights activists disagree over what testing is acceptable. The cures for polio and diabetes, for example, were found through research that used animals to test for lifesaving medicine and to gather knowledge about biological processes. Without more animal testing research, we might never find a cure for AIDS or cancer. Developing new treatments for diseases has been so beneficial for sick human beings that most people feel animal testing was worth it. Others feel that we have no right to kill an animal, no matter how great the benefits.

Whatever you believe, there's no doubt that careful procedures and sharing information can safely reduce the number of animals used.

The Food and Drug Administration actually requires testing on animals for the development of all new drugs and new ingredients or combinations of ingredients to be used or eaten by humans. In some cases the animal tests may not be very extensive—but animals are used. Researchers in companies and at universities are trying to develop more non-animal tests, but it may be years before these become widely accepted as standard procedure. We give companies credit for investing in research on alternatives. CEP recommends you seek out and read information on all sides of this issue.

The animal protection movement has raised public awareness about the use of animals for safety testing, especially for cosmetics and household products. Giant companies such as Revlon and Avon have publicly committed to end animal testing for their products. L'Oreal and Procter & Gamble have made impressive strides to reduce the numbers of animals necessary for testing. All of these and many other companies have committed substantial amounts of money to investigating alternatives to animal testing. With the founding of the Johns Hopkins Center for Alternatives to Animal Testing 10 years ago, and other research centers dedicated to developing alternatives, some tests which relied on animals have been replaced with non-animal tests.

For every animal suffering due to testing, millions of animals suffer from birth to slaughter through factory farming—the raising, transport, and slaughter of animals on factory farms. Read the Factory Farming EXTRA to learn more about this issue.

Because animal testing is such a controversial issue, the EXTRAS section not only explains which companies are testing, but also identifies those that have demonstrated a commitment to research and/or use alternatives. An EXTRA for animal testing is not given if a company does no testing. Companies that still conduct tests on animals received one of six messages:

1) ANIMAL TESTING: NON-MEDICAL PURPOSES

These are companies that manufacture no medical products yet test their products on animals. They make such products as cosmetics or industrial chemicals. Humans come into contact with these chemicals, especially workers at industrial plants. In the last five years, the companies in this group have not reported any effort to reduce the number of animals they use and/or spent significant resources ($250,000 or more annually) researching alternative testing methods.

2) ANIMAL TESTING: MEDICAL PURPOSES

These drug/pharmaceutical makers conduct tests on animals. Like those in the above category, these companies have neither significantly reduced the numbers of animals they use (by 40% or more) nor substantially contributed to the advancement of alternative research methods (zero to under $250,000 annually) over the last five years.

3) ANIMAL TESTING: MEDICAL AND NON-MEDICAL PURPOSES

These companies perform tests for both medical and non-medical products. Like those in the above category, these companies have neither significantly reduced the numbers of animals they use (by 40% or more) nor substantially contributed to the advancement of alternative research methods (zero to under $250,000 each year) over the last five years.

4) ANIMAL TESTING: NON-MEDICAL PURPOSES, SIGNIFICANT ALTERNATIVE EFFORTS

Although these companies test on animals for products that do not serve a medical purpose, they have reduced the numbers of animals tested by at least 40% over the last five years and/or made financial commitments of $250,000 annually or more to explore alternative test options.

5) ANIMAL TESTING: MEDICAL PURPOSES, SIGNIFICANT ALTERNATIVE EFFORTS

These companies conduct research on animals to further medical knowledge but, unlike those in category two, have reduced the number of animals used by at least 40% over the last five years and/or donated $250,000 annually to researching alternative testing methods.

6) ANIMAL TESTING: MEDICAL AND NON-MEDICAL PURPOSES, SIGNIFICANT ALTERNATIVE EFFORTS

These companies perform tests for both medical and non-medical products. They have reduced the numbers of animals tested by at least 40% over the last five years and/or made financial commitments of $250,000 annually or more to explore alternative test options.

For companies with any of these EXTRAS, there may be some adjustment made for company size.

To find out about how to start an animal protection club at your school, or just to learn more about animal welfare issues, contact the National Association for Humane and Environmental Education, the youth education division of The Humane Society of the United States, 2100 L Street, NW, Washington, DC 20037. They offer information about fur issues, dissection in schools, animal testing, factory farming, and many environmental issues as well.

100% profit to charity. Newman's Own, Inc., the natural food company founded by actor Paul Newman, donates every penny of profits—more than $55 million since 1982—to charities. One of the most well-known of the 400 groups is the Hole-in-the-Wall Gang Camp for children with life-threatening illnesses. Mr. Newman and a friend started the camp so that kids who have to spend a lot of time in the hospital could also enjoy the outdoors, free of charge.

CERES Principles. In 1989 the Exxon oil tanker Valdez ran aground in Alaska and spilled more than 10 million gallons of oil into the ocean. The worst oil spill in American history, it killed thousands of otters, seals, fish, and birds and destroyed the homes of many other species. After this disaster, the Coalition for Environmentally Responsible Economies (CERES) wrote the Valdez Principles, now called the CERES Principles. The Principles are 10 commitments to a healthy environment. CERES urges all corporations to sign. The Principles do not monitor specific things a company has to do—so a company might sign and not necessarily follow the Principles. As of mid-1992, there were 48 members (including CEP), none among the Fortune 1000 companies.

These are the CERES Principles: 1)protection of the biosphere 2)sustainable use of natural resources 3)reduction and disposal of wastes 4)wise use of energy 5)risk reduction 6)marketing of safe products and services 7)damage compensation 8)disclosure 9)environmental directors and managers 10)an annual environmental audit.

Cigarettes. The five major U.S. producers of cigarettes are RJR Nabisco, Philip Morris, American Brands, Loews, and U.S. Tobacco. You may have noticed that, although we include food products made by two of these companies, RJR Nabisco and Philip Morris, in this guide, we do not list cigarettes. The Council on Economic Priorities considers manufacturing and promoting cigarettes (which are responsible for an estimated 1,000 deaths a day in the U.S. alone) unethical because smoking is a direct and major threat to public health. These addictive products are aggressively marketed by producers, especially to women, minorities, and youth. Health officials and consumer activists have objected for years to billboard advertising in poorer urban neighborhoods where, they claim, people are dying in disproportionate numbers from diseases related to smoking. Also, recent advertising campaigns using cartoon characters to market cigarettes have been criticized strongly. (See Chapter Three.)

As anti-smoking groups work to ban all print and outdoor cigarette ads, the tobacco industry is shifting to direct marketing, such as mail offers, magazines, posters, and sponsorship of televised sporting events. They are also putting their sales efforts into countries where regulations are few and health warnings are often not required.

Corporate Conscience Awards/Dishonorable Corporate Conscience Awards. Each year CEP honors companies for outstanding records in environmentalism, charity, equal opportunity for minorities and women, community action, and meeting the needs of employees. Outside experts, CEP staff, and the companies themselves suggest nominees. We also invite you, our readers, to nominate particularly terrific companies you may know about. Just write us a note or call (212)420-1133 for a nomination form.

An independent panel of judges chooses the winners. CEP holds an awards dinner and ceremony in New York with celebrity emcees. In 1992 our host was Mike Wallace and the winning corporations were Church & Dwight, US West, General Mills, Prudential Insurance, Supermarkets General, Donnelly Corp., Tom's of Maine, Lotus, and Conservatree.

Companies with poor track records in these same social issues get CEP's Dishonorable Mentions. 1992's unlucky winners were DuPont, MAXXAM, and RJR Nabisco.

Factory Farming. Most of the chicken and meat we eat in this country comes from huge, modern farms that are more like animal factories than a family farm. Companies that produce this kind of meat claim in advertisements that their animals are comfortable and healthy. Unfortunately, that is not always true.

Chickens, for example, usually have less than one square foot of living space per bird. Such crowded conditions lead to more disease. The U.S. Department of Agriculture believes that about one-third of all raw poultry now carries salmonella or campylobacter bacteria. Another problem is that chickens are bred for weight. They get so heavy for their bone size that their legs become crippled and painful.

Veal calves are also overcrowded, kept in narrow stalls too small to turn around in. Fed a liquid diet without enough iron, they're prone to anemia and lower resistance to disease—just so they'll have a light flesh color that's supposed to be more appealing to eat. The sick veal calves are given antibiotics and then quickly slaughtered, so some drugs wind up in the veal people eat.

Factory farming, or agribusiness, not only hurts the animals themselves—it can hurt the whole environment in a lot of different ways, including the following:

- Factory farming depends on fossil fuels, the single largest cause of global warming.
- Clearing away parts of the rainforest for livestock pasture and feed crops produces excess carbon dioxide, part of the global warming problem.
- The excrement of billions of farm animals produces methane, another reason for global warming as well as the destruction of the ozone layer.
- Chemical fertilizers produce nitrous oxide, again part of global warming.
- Excrement, pesticides, and fertilizers cause fresh-water pollution or acid rain.
- More than half of the total amount of water we use in this country is for raising livestock, according to some estimates.

If you feel that factory farming needs to be changed, there are several actions you can take. You can ask for vegetarian meals at restaurants and especially at fast-food chains. You can convince your school cafeteria or camp to offer healthy meatless entrees. You can write to companies that sell meat to request that farms use more humane, more ecologically sound methods. In other words, a system that doesn't depend on antibiotics, hormones, pesticides, genetically engineered animals, herbicides, and overcrowding.

Fair Share. Fair Share, a program of the NAACP, was begun in 1981 to help corporate America return dollars spent by black Americans to the communities from which they originate. Fair Share companies agree to increase economic opportunity for minorities. Specifically, Fair Share promotes:

- Minority vendor programs for purchases of goods and services from blacks contractors, professionals, and financial and insurance institutions.
- Aggressive affirmative action programs and opportunities for the advancement of blacks into senior management positions.
- Representation of blacks on corporate boards.
- Philanthropic contributions to worthy black organizations and causes.

Foreign-based Company. CEP asks for women's advancement and environmental information for the worldwide operations of foreign-based companies. But for minority advancement we use information about U.S. operations only, because the definition of a minority changes as one crosses borders and because information on overseas operations is difficult to get. Even using these rules, foreign companies are a challenge for social responsibility researchers. In many issues, the United States and foreign countries have dramatically different standards. For example, because there are far fewer women in the top levels of management of Japanese companies, a company that rates highly by Japanese standards on this issue would not do as well using American criteria. We tried to apply our usual criteria to these foreign-based companies, so keep in mind that many might rate better within their own countries.

Infant Formula. There are serious ethical problems with marketing infant formula to parents who do not know how to use it correctly. In 1981, the World Health Organization (WHO) and UNICEF developed an international code which regulates the marketing and distribution of breast milk substitutes. Many infant formula companies violate parts of this code. We note the companies which violate the following:

1) The distribution of free or low-priced samples directly to parents is strictly prohibited. Why? Because using infant formula properly requires training and education, and free samples rarely are given out with either. Mothers receive the samples, try them out, and just about the time that the sample runs out, they discover that their bodies are no longer making breast milk. (If a woman stops breast feeding, her body stops producing milk.) So, mothers become dependent on this very expensive product and, if they are poor, dilute the formula to make it last longer. This can be dangerous for two reasons: a)dilution lowers the nutritional value of each serving of formula, and continual "watering down" can cause malnutrition; b)in areas with poor water conditions, the water is often contaminated, and babies become sick when they drink it. The free sample problem has occurred most in developing countries, but it happens everywhere. WHO/UNICEF have urged the major infant formula companies to stop free distribution of samples by the end of 1992, but it is unlikely that it will happen.

2) Advertising infant formula to the public on television, in supermarkets, in magazines, via posters, or through coupons is prohibited by WHO. Encouraging parents to buy a food product for their baby with flashy phrases and colorful pictures causes problems when training and edu-

cation are not included and when the nutrition of the child is at stake. Mothers should make the decision to use breast milk substitute with their doctors at the hospital, not in aisle four at the supermarket surrounded by ads.

Nuclear Weapons. Company has nuclear weapons-related contract(s) of any amount. These may include contracts for nuclear weapons or their components; and/or systems aiding launch, guidance, delivery or deployment of nuclear weapons.

Pesticides. Pesticides, chemicals which kill the natural enemies of crops, help farmers save crops. On the other hand, pesticides cause problems. These powerful chemicals are washed by rainwater from farmland into rivers and eventually into our drinking water. They can be harmful, even deadly, to farmworkers who apply them without the right protection. Small amounts of pesticides can stay on fruits and vegetables we eat. Out of 729 pesticides that the Environmental Protection Agency knows of, only a tiny number can be detected by the Food and Drug Administration. Luckily, farmers have some alternatives to pesticides—organic or biological methods of pest control.

Small Companies. You may wonder why CEP included small businesses—companies with fewer than 100 employees—along with corporate giants with hundreds of thousands of employees. Not only do small companies make up 98.9% of all U.S. companies, but they also lead the way in innovative management, use of products that are organically grown and "cruelty-free," and responsiveness to employees and consumers.

In 1991, none of the 17 small companies CEP studied had military or nuclear power contracts, or ties to South Africa. Not only do they avoid animal testing, they tend to be strong advocates for animal welfare. Many small companies recycle raw materials, use recyclable packaging, and minimize use of toxic chemicals.

Some small businesses, especially those with a majority of female employees, offer a flexible work schedule: employees may work at home, work part-time or on alternative schedules, or bring infants to work with them. Companies report that these arrangements don't cost much. In fact, higher morale and lower turnover often result.

CEP has considered the size and structure of a company when determining our ratings. Of the more than three million companies with fewer than 20 employees, an estimated 200,000 have sprung up just in the last four or five years. It's usually hard enough for such small companies to keep afloat financially, so generous contributions to the community or minority advancement may be especially difficult. In a few cases, however, these issues are given top consideration from the very beginning.

South Africa. After the release of Nelson Mandela in 1990, it looked as if South Africa's apartheid—the systematic segregation of and discrimination against blacks—was definitely going to end under President F.W. de Klerk's leadership. Three important laws that discriminated against black South Africans were repealed. President Bush lifted the U.S. Comprehensive Anti-Apartheid Act of 1986, which prevented American companies from making new investments in South Africa or deducting taxes paid to South Africa from their U.S. tax bill. The lifting of these economic sanctions disappointed some activists who believe that until black South Africans are allowed to vote and until there is a new constitution, doing business in South Africa is socially irresponsible.

In 1992, events in South Africa took a turn for the worse when 50 men, women, and children were killed in an attack. Eyewitnesses claimed that South African police supplied the killers with weapons. Because of this violence, anti-apartheid groups have been less willing to negotiate with the de Klerk government.

The whole question of whether or not an American company hurts or helps apartheid by either investing or operating in South Africa is very complicated. Some companies say they are helping to end apartheid by giving blacks jobs, benefits, and other services that white South Africans would not provide. But others say that until all South Africans can vote, the country is still oppressing most of its citizens. So to invest in South Africa is unacceptable.

Teen Programs and Scholarships. Corporations often donate money to charities or set up health, art, or educational programs. This EXTRA means a company has made a real commitment, in terms of time, money, and resources, to helping young people. Stride Rite, the shoe company that makes Keds, gives 5% of its pre-tax profits to fund programs such as the Cambridge Volunteers. Employees volunteer their time to work with students who are considered at risk for dropping out. Stride Rite also funds a Public Service Program which gives grants, prizes, book allowances, loan deferrals, and work-study money to students who choose low-paying public service jobs.

Workplace Principles. The Workplace Principles were developed in 1988 by the Citizens Commission on AIDS to highlight HIV/AIDS as a crucial issue in employee rights. The 10 principles cover HIV/AIDS policies for the workplace. Companies pledge not to discriminate against workers with AIDS, to educate all employees about how AIDS is spread (and how it isn't), to keep medical records confidential, and to not require HIV screening as part of hiring practices.

CHAPTER 8

Shopping for your future

Ratings by Company

SHOPPING FOR YOUR FUTURE: RATINGS BY COMPANY

HONOR ROLL AND UNDERACHIEVERS

We thought you'd be interested in an easy-to-use list of the highest rated companies in the book, our Honor Roll—and then the lowest rated, our Underachievers. Please remember that these companies were ranked high or low ONLY BASED ON THE ISSUE AREAS COVERED IN THIS GUIDE! THE ISSUES TEENAGERS SAID WERE MOST IMPORTANT. That means it's possible that a company we rate as one of the best in our four issues could be really terrible when it comes to giving to charity. Or a company could have a very bad record in the environment, minority and women's advancement, and disclosure of information BUT have a fantastic record for labor relations.

To make the Honor Roll, a company had to have three or more As and no Fs or Incompletes. Our Underachievers had two more Fs than As—and we had grades for at least three out of the four issue areas for them.

You will notice that there are almost the same number of large companies on the Honor Roll and the Underachievers list. But there are additional small companies on the Honor Roll. Why? Because CEP deliberately tries to research small companies that have outstanding social records in the first place.

So here at a glance are the Honor Roll and the Underachievers:

THE HONOR ROLL

Anheuser-Busch
Aroma Vera
Aveda Corp.
Avon Products, Inc.
Ben & Jerry's
Birkenstock Footprint Sandals Inc.
Body Love Natural Cosmetics
Body Shop, The
Campbell Soup
Carter Hawley Hale Store, Inc.
Clorox
Coca-Cola Company
Colgate-Palmolive
Dayton Hudson
Ecco Bella
Esprit de Corp
General Mills
Johnson & Johnson
Kellogg Company
Kiss My Face
Minn. Mining & Mfg. (3M)
Newman's Own
Nordstrom, Inc.
Orjene Natural Cosmetics
PepsiCo, Inc.
Quaker Oats Company
Rachel Perry, Inc.
Rhino Records, Inc.
Seventh Generation
Sony Corp.
Stonyfield Farm, Inc.
Time Warner Inc.
Tom's of Maine

UNDERACHIEVERS

Brunswick Corporation
Carter-Wallace
ConAgra
Imasco Limited
Pfizer Inc.
RJR Nabisco, Inc.
Reebok International Ltd.
Russell Corp.
Sun Company, Inc.
Texaco Inc.
USX Corporation
United Biscuits
Wm. Wrigley Jr. Company

COMPANIES	ENVIRONMENT	MINORITIES	WOMEN	DISCLOSURE
ADIDAS	I	I	I	F

PRODUCTS OR SUBSIDIARIES Adidas

EXTRAS Foreign company

ADDRESS c/o Adidas USA Inc.
15 Independence Blvd.
Warren, NJ 07059
Peter Pirner, CEO

COMPANIES	ENVIRONMENT	MINORITIES	WOMEN	DISCLOSURE
AL COPELAND ENTERPRISES	I	I	I	F

PRODUCTS OR SUBSIDIARIES Church's Chicken, Popeye's Famous Fried Chicken & Biscuits

EXTRAS Factory farming

ADDRESS 1333 S. Clearview Pkwy.
Jefferson, LA 70121
(800) 222-5857
Al Copeland, Chairman and CEO

COMPANIES	ENVIRONMENT	MINORITIES	WOMEN	DISCLOSURE
ALADAN	I	I	I	F

PRODUCTS OR SUBSIDIARIES Embrace, Gold Circle Coin, Rainbow, Saxon

ADDRESS P.O. Box 8308
Dothan, AL 36303
Julian Danielly, President

COMPANIES	ENVIRONMENT	MINORITIES	WOMEN	DISCLOSURE
ALBERTO-CULVER	C	F	A	A

PRODUCTS OR SUBSIDIARIES — Alberto, Alberto VO5, Command, Consort deodorant, Consort Hair Spray, Consort Styling Mousse, Get Set, TCB

EXTRAS — Animal testing: non-medical purposes

ADDRESS — 2525 Armitage Ave.
Melrose Park, IL 60160
Leonard H. Lavin, Chairman & CEO

COMPANIES	ENVIRONMENT	MINORITIES	WOMEN	DISCLOSURE
ALLIED-LYONS	C	C	C	A

PRODUCTS OR SUBSIDIARIES — Baskin Robbins 31, Brink, Dunkin Donuts, Haust, Lyons, Maryland Cookies, Mister Donut

EXTRAS — Foreign company

ADDRESS — 24 Portland Pl.
London, England W1N 4BB
Derrick Holden-Brown, Chairman of the Board

COMPANIES	ENVIRONMENT	MINORITIES	WOMEN	DISCLOSURE
AMERICAN HOME PRODUCTS	F	F	C	A

PRODUCTS OR SUBSIDIARIES — Compound W, Crunch'n'Munch, Denorex, Jiffy Pop, Maypo Oatmeal, Wheatena

EXTRAS — Animal testing: medical & non-medical purposes, significant alternative efforts; Infant formula; Indirect ties to South Africa

ADDRESS — 685 Third Ave.
New York, NY 10017-4085
John R. Stafford, Chairman & CEO

COMPANIES	ENVIRONMENT	MINORITIES	WOMEN	DISCLOSURE
AMOCO	F	C	C	A

PRODUCTS OR SUBSIDIARIES: Amoco

EXTRAS: Animal testing: medical & non-medical purposes; Corporate Conscience Award - Community

ADDRESS: 200 E. Randolph Dr.
Chicago, IL 60601-6404
(800) 333-3991
H. Lawrence Fuller, Chairman & CEO

COMPANIES	ENVIRONMENT	MINORITIES	WOMEN	DISCLOSURE
ANHEUSER-BUSCH	C	A	A	A

PRODUCTS OR SUBSIDIARIES: Break Cakes, Colonial, Eagle Snacks, Earth Grains, Rainbo

ADDRESS: One Busch Pl.
St. Louis, MO 63118
August A. Busch III, Chairman & President

COMPANIES	ENVIRONMENT	MINORITIES	WOMEN	DISCLOSURE
AROMA VERA	A	A	A	A

PRODUCTS OR SUBSIDIARIES: Aroma Vera

EXTRAS: Small company

ADDRESS: 3384 S. Robertson Pl.
Los Angeles, CA 90034
Marcel Lavabre, Chairman & CEO

COMPANIES	ENVIRONMENT	MINORITIES	WOMEN	DISCLOSURE
ATLANTIC RICHFIELD	F	C	A	C

PRODUCTS OR SUBSIDIARIES: ARCO

EXTRAS: Animal testing: non-medical purposes

ADDRESS: 515 South Flower St.
Los Angeles, CA 90071
(800) 322-2726
Lodwrick M. Cook, Chairman & CEO

COMPANIES	ENVIRONMENT	MINORITIES	WOMEN	DISCLOSURE
AVEDA	A	A	A	A

PRODUCTS OR SUBSIDIARIES: Aveda Purefumes, Aveda hair and skin care

EXTRAS: CERES Principles

ADDRESS: 4000 Pheasant Ridge Dr.
Blaine, MN 55449
(800) 328-0849
Horst Rechelbacher, Chairman & CEO

COMPANIES	ENVIRONMENT	MINORITIES	WOMEN	DISCLOSURE
AVERY DENNISON	I	I	C	F

PRODUCTS OR SUBSIDIARIES: Aigner, Avery, Carter's, Dennison, Glue-Stic, K & M Notebooks

ADDRESS: 150 North Orange Grove Blvd.
Pasadena, CA 91103
(800) 292-8379
Charles D. Miller, Chairman & CEO

COMPANIES	ENVIRONMENT	MINORITIES	WOMEN	DISCLOSURE
AVON	C	A	A	A

PRODUCTS OR SUBSIDIARIES: Avon, Bioadvance, Charisma, Clear Skin II, Cool Confidence, Daily Revival, Fancy Feet, Feelin' Fresh, Giorgio, Silver Lights, Simply Brilliant, Skin-So-Soft, Soft Essentials, Sun Seekers

EXTRAS: Corporate Conscience Award - Equal Employment Opportunity

ADDRESS: 9 W. 57th St.
New York, NY 10019
(800) 858-8000
James E. Preston, Chairman & CEO

COMPANIES	ENVIRONMENT	MINORITIES	WOMEN	DISCLOSURE
BEN & JERRY'S	A	C	A	A

PRODUCTS OR SUBSIDIARIES: Ben & Jerry's

EXTRAS: CERES Principles; Corporate Conscience Award - Charity; Workplace Principles

ADDRESS: Rt. 100, P .O. Box 240
Waterbury, VT 05676-0240
Chuck Lacy, President & CEO

COMPANIES	ENVIRONMENT	MINORITIES	WOMEN	DISCLOSURE
BENETTON GROUP	I	I	I	F

PRODUCTS OR SUBSIDIARIES: Benetton clothing, Benetton stores, Colors de Benetton

EXTRAS: Foreign company

ADDRESS: 55 E. 59th St.
New York, NY 10022
Luciano Benetton, President

COMPANIES	ENVIRONMENT	MINORITIES	WOMEN	DISCLOSURE
BERTELSMANN	I	I	I	F

PRODUCTS OR SUBSIDIARIES: Arista Records, BMG Music, RCA Records

EXTRAS: Foreign company

ADDRESS: 1133 Ave. of the Americas
New York, NY 10036
Peter Olson, President

COMPANIES	ENVIRONMENT	MINORITIES	WOMEN	DISCLOSURE
SOCIETE BIC	I	I	I	F

PRODUCTS OR SUBSIDIARIES: Bic

EXTRAS: Foreign company

ADDRESS: 500 Bic Dr.
Milford, CT 06460
(800) 597-4950
Ray Winter, President & CEO

COMPANIES	ENVIRONMENT	MINORITIES	WOMEN	DISCLOSURE
BIRKENSTOCK FOOTPRINT SANDALS	A	C	A	A

PRODUCTS OR SUBSIDIARIES: Birkenstock Footprint Sandals

ADDRESS: 8171 Redwood Blvd.
Novato, CA 94945
(800) 487-2475
Margot Fraser, President & CEO

COMPANIES	ENVIRONMENT	MINORITIES	WOMEN	DISCLOSURE
BODY LOVE NATURAL COSMETICS	A	A	A	A

PRODUCTS OR SUBSIDIARIES: Amazing Grains, Aroma Lotion, Aroma Oil, Herbal Facial Steams, Juniper Tonic Massage Oil, Love Mitts

EXTRAS: Small company

ADDRESS: P.O. Box 7542
Santa Cruz, CA 95061
Elizabeth Jones, President & CEO

COMPANIES	ENVIRONMENT	MINORITIES	WOMEN	DISCLOSURE
THE BODY SHOP	A	C	A	A

PRODUCTS OR SUBSIDIARIES: Body Shop makeup and skin care, Body Shop perfume, Body Shop shampoo

EXTRAS: Foreign company

ADDRESS: Hanover Technical Center
45 Horsehill Rd.
Cedar Knolls, NJ 07927-2003
David Edward, President

COMPANIES	ENVIRONMENT	MINORITIES	WOMEN	DISCLOSURE
BORDEN	F	A	C	A

PRODUCTS OR SUBSIDIARIES Borden Ice Cream, Borden Juice, Bravo, Buckeye, Cain's, Campfire, Cary's, Cheez Doodles, Chesty, Clover Club, Cottage Fries, Cracker Jacks, Crane's, Dipsy Doodles, Eagle Brand, El Molino, Elmer's, Fisher, Geiser's, Guy's, Jays, KAS, Krazy Glue, Krunchers!, La Famous, Lite-line, Little Panchos, MacDonald's, Meadow Gold, Moore's, Mountain High, New York Deli, Old Fashioned Recipe, Pepitos, Ranch Fries, Red Seal, Ridgie's, Seyferts, Snacktime, Thirstee Smash, Turtles, Vermont Maple, Viva frozen yogurt, Viva yogurt, Wise

EXTRAS Direct investment in South Africa

ADDRESS 180 East Broad St., 25th fl.
Columbus, OH 43215
Anthony D'Amato, Chairman & CEO

COMPANIES	ENVIRONMENT	MINORITIES	WOMEN	DISCLOSURE
BRISTOL-MYERS SQUIBB	C	A	C	A

PRODUCTS OR SUBSIDIARIES Ammens, Ban, Clairol, Final Net, Fostex, Herbal Essence, Infusium 23, Instant Beauty, Keri Lotion, PreSun, Sea Breeze

EXTRAS Animal testing: medical & non-medical purposes, significant alternative efforts; Direct investment in South Africa; Infant formula; Workplace Principles

ADDRESS 345 Park Ave.
New York, NY 10154
(800) 332-2056
Richard L. Gelb, Chairman & CEO

COMPANIES	ENVIRONMENT	MINORITIES	WOMEN	DISCLOSURE
BRITISH PETROLEUM	F	F	C	A

PRODUCTS OR SUBSIDIARIES: BP America

EXTRAS: Animal testing: non-medical purposes, significant alternative efforts; Direct investment in South Africa; Foreign company; Workplace Principles

ADDRESS: c/o BP America
200 Public Square
Cleveland, OH 44114
Rodney F. Chase, President & CEO

BROWN GROUP	I	I	F	F

PRODUCTS OR SUBSIDIARIES: Air Step, Brown, Buster Brown, Naturalizer, Regal

ADDRESS: 8400 Maryland Ave.
St. Louis, MO 63166
(800) 766-6465
B. A. Bridewater, Jr., Chairman & CEO

BRUNSWICK	F	I	C	F

PRODUCTS OR SUBSIDIARIES: Brunswick

EXTRAS: Nuclear weapons

ADDRESS: One Brunswick Plaza
Skokie, IL 60077-1089
Jack F. Reichert, Chairman, President & CEO

COMPANIES	ENVIRONMENT	MINORITIES	WOMEN	DISCLOSURE
BUGLE BOY	I	I	I	F

PRODUCTS OR SUBSIDIARIES: Bugle Boy

ADDRESS: 2900 Madera Rd.
Simi Valley, CA 93065
William Mow, Chairman & CEO

COMPANIES	ENVIRONMENT	MINORITIES	WOMEN	DISCLOSURE
CADBURY SCHWEPPES	A	I	C	A

PRODUCTS OR SUBSIDIARIES: Bassett, Beechnut, Cadbury, Canada Dry, Crush, Eclairs, Mott's, Murray, Schweppes, Sunkist

EXTRAS: Foreign company

ADDRESS: 6 High Ridge Park
Stamford, CT 06905-0800
Frank Swan, President & CEO

COMPANIES	ENVIRONMENT	MINORITIES	WOMEN	DISCLOSURE
CAMPBELL SOUP	C	A	A	A

PRODUCTS OR SUBSIDIARIES: Godiva, La Croix, Pepperidge Farm, V8

EXTRAS: Animal testing: non-medical purposes, significant alternative efforts

ADDRESS: Campbell Pl.
Camden, NJ 08103-1799
(800) 257-8443
David W. Johnson, President & CEO

COMPANIES	ENVIRONMENT	MINORITIES	WOMEN	DISCLOSURE
CARTER HAWLEY HALE STORES	A	C	A	A

PRODUCTS OR SUBSIDIARIES
Emporium, The Broadway, The Broadway Southwest, Weinstocks

ADDRESS
444 S. Flower St.
Los Angeles, CA 90071
Philip M. Hawley, Chairman & CEO

COMPANIES	ENVIRONMENT	MINORITIES	WOMEN	DISCLOSURE
CARTER-WALLACE	C	I	F	F

PRODUCTS OR SUBSIDIARIES
Arrid, Lady's Choice, Linco Beer, Mentor, Nair, Poker, Rilacrin, Sea & Ski, Sue Pree, Trojan

EXTRAS
Animal testing: medical purposes only

ADDRESS
c/o Ruder-Finn
301 E. 57th St.
New York, NY 10022
Henry H. Hoyt, Jr., Chairman & CEO

COMPANIES	ENVIRONMENT	MINORITIES	WOMEN	DISCLOSURE
CARVEL	I	I	I	F

PRODUCTS OR SUBSIDIARIES
Carvel

ADDRESS
20 Batterson Park Rd.
Farmington, CT 06032-2502
Steve Fellingham, CEO

COMPANIES	ENVIRONMENT	MINORITIES	WOMEN	DISCLOSURE
CHEVRON	F	A	F	A

PRODUCTS OR SUBSIDIARIES	Chevron
EXTRAS	Animal testing: non-medical purposes, significant alternative efforts; Direct investment in South Africa; Pesticides; Workplace Principles
ADDRESS	575 Market St., Room 878 San Francisco, CA 94105 Kenneth T. Derr, Chairman & CEO

COMPANIES	ENVIRONMENT	MINORITIES	WOMEN	DISCLOSURE
CHURCH & DWIGHT	A	C	C	A

PRODUCTS OR SUBSIDIARIES	Arm & Hammer
EXTRAS	Animal testing: non-medical purposes, significant alternative efforts; Corporate Conscience Award-Environment
ADDRESS	469 N. Harrison St. Princeton, NJ 08543 Dwight C. Minton, Chairman & CEO

COMPANIES	ENVIRONMENT	MINORITIES	WOMEN	DISCLOSURE
CLOROX	A	A	C	A

PRODUCTS OR SUBSIDIARIES	Deer Park
EXTRAS	Animal testing: non-medical purposes, significant alternative efforts
ADDRESS	P.O. Box 24305 Oakland, CA 94623-1305 Craig Sullivan, CEO

COMPANIES	ENVIRONMENT	MINORITIES	WOMEN	DISCLOSURE
COCA-COLA	C	A	A	A

PRODUCTS OR SUBSIDIARIES — Bright & Early, Coca-Cola, Fanta, Five Alive, Fresca, Hi-C, Mello Yello, Minute Maid, Mr. Pibb, Ramblin' Root Beer, Sprite, Tab

EXTRAS — Indirect ties to South Africa; Teen programs & scholarships; Workplace Principles

ADDRESS — P.O. Drawer 1734
Atlanta, GA 30301
(800) 438-2653
Roberto C. Goizueta, Chairman & CEO

COMPANIES	ENVIRONMENT	MINORITIES	WOMEN	DISCLOSURE
COLGATE-PALMOLIVE	A	A	A	A

PRODUCTS OR SUBSIDIARIES — Afta Skin Conditioner, Baby Magic shampoo, Baby Magic skin care, Balm Barr, Brushless Shave, Colgate shaving cream, Colgate toothbrushes, Colgate toothpaste, Flourigard, Hawk After Shave, Irish Spring deodorant, Irish Spring soap, Lather Shave, Medicated Face Conditioner, Mennen, Millionaire After Shave, Palmolive, Peak, Protein 21, Skin Bracer, Sof' Stroke, Softsoap, Teen Spirit, Ultra Brite, Wildroot

EXTRAS — Animal testing: medical & non-medical purposes, significant alternative efforts; Direct investment in South Africa

ADDRESS — 300 Park Ave.
New York, NY 10022
Reuben Mark, Chairman, President & CEO

COMPANIES	ENVIRONMENT	MINORITIES	WOMEN	DISCLOSURE
CONAGRA	F	I	C	F

PRODUCTS OR SUBSIDIARIES: Orville Redenbacher's, Swiss Miss Cocoa

EXTRAS: Dishonorable Corporate Conscience Award; Factory farming

ADDRESS: One ConAgra Dr.
Omaha, NE 68102-5001
Phil Fletcher, Chairman & CEO

COMPANIES	ENVIRONMENT	MINORITIES	WOMEN	DISCLOSURE
A.T.CROSS	I	I	F	F

PRODUCTS OR SUBSIDIARIES: Cross pens & pencils

ADDRESS: One Albion Rd.
Lincoln, RI 02865-3700
(800) 282-7677
Bradford R. Boss, Chairman & CEO

COMPANIES	ENVIRONMENT	MINORITIES	WOMEN	DISCLOSURE
DWG CORP.	I	I	C	F

PRODUCTS OR SUBSIDIARIES: Arby's

EXTRAS: Factory farming

ADDRESS: 6917 Collins Ave.
Miami, FL 33161
Victor Posner, Chairman, President & CEO

COMPANIES	ENVIRONMENT	MINORITIES	WOMEN	DISCLOSURE
DAYTON HUDSON	A	A	A	A

PRODUCTS OR SUBSIDIARIES: Dayton's, Hudson's, Marshall Field's, Mervyn's, Target

EXTRAS: Corporate Conscience Award-Charity

ADDRESS: 777 Nicollet Mall
Minneapolis, MN 55402
Kenneth A. Macke, Chairman & CEO

COMPANIES	ENVIRONMENT	MINORITIES	WOMEN	DISCLOSURE
DERBY INTERNATIONAL	I	I	I	F

PRODUCTS OR SUBSIDIARIES: Haro, Nishiki, Raleigh

EXTRAS: Foreign company

ADDRESS: c/o Derby Cycle Corporation
22710 72nd Ave. S.
Kent, WA 98032
(800) 222-5527
Chuck Wilky, CEO

COMPANIES	ENVIRONMENT	MINORITIES	WOMEN	DISCLOSURE
DOLE FOOD	C	C	C	A

PRODUCTS OR SUBSIDIARIES: Dole juice, Dole nuts, Fruit 'n Juice

ADDRESS: 31355 Oak Crest Dr.
Westlake Village, CA 91361
David H. Murdock, Chairman & CEO

COMPANIES	ENVIRONMENT	MINORITIES	WOMEN	DISCLOSURE
DOMINO'S PIZZA	A	A	C	C

PRODUCTS OR SUBSIDIARIES: Domino's Pizza

ADDRESS: P.O. Box 997
Ann Arbor, MI 48106
Thomas S. Monaghan, Chairman & CEO

COMPANIES	ENVIRONMENT	MINORITIES	WOMEN	DISCLOSURE
DREYER'S GRAND ICE CREAM	I	I	F	F

PRODUCTS OR SUBSIDIARIES: Dreyer's, Edy's

ADDRESS: 5929 College Ave.
Oakland, CA 94618
(800) 888-3442
T. Gary Rogers, Chairman & CEO

COMPANIES	ENVIRONMENT	MINORITIES	WOMEN	DISCLOSURE
EASTMAN KODAK	F	A	A	A

PRODUCTS OR SUBSIDIARIES: Stri-dex, PHiso-Derm, Tussy

EXTRAS: Animal testing: medical and non-medical purposes, significant alternative efforts; Corporate Conscience Award - EEO

ADDRESS: 343 State St.
Rochester, NY 14650
Kay Whitmore, Chairman & CEO

COMPANIES	ENVIRONMENT	MINORITIES	WOMEN	DISCLOSURE
ECCO BELLA	A	C	A	A

PRODUCTS OR SUBSIDIARIES: Ecco Bella

EXTRAS: Small company

ADDRESS: 125 Pompton Plains Crossroads
Wayne, NJ 07470
(800) 322-9366
Sally Malanga, President

COMPANIES	ENVIRONMENT	MINORITIES	WOMEN	DISCLOSURE
ESMARK APPAREL	I	I	I	F

PRODUCTS OR SUBSIDIARIES: Danskin

ADDRESS: 111 W. 40th St. 18th fl.
New York, NY 10018
(800) 288-6749
Byron Hero, Chairman & CEO

COMPANIES	ENVIRONMENT	MINORITIES	WOMEN	DISCLOSURE
ESPRIT DE CORP	A	A	A	A

PRODUCTS OR SUBSIDIARIES Esprit, Susie Tompkins

ADDRESS 900 Minnesota St.
San Francisco, CA 94107
Fritz Ammann, President & CEO

COMPANIES	ENVIRONMENT	MINORITIES	WOMEN	DISCLOSURE
ESTEE LAUDER	A	I	A	C

PRODUCTS OR SUBSIDIARIES Aramis, Clinique, Estee Lauder, Origins, Prescriptives, White Linen

EXTRAS Direct investment in South Africa

ADDRESS 767 Fifth Ave.
New York, NY 10153
Leonard Lauder, President & CEO

COMPANIES	ENVIRONMENT	MINORITIES	WOMEN	DISCLOSURE
EXXON CORP.	F	C	C	A

PRODUCTS OR SUBSIDIARIES Exxon

EXTRAS Animal testing: non-medical purposes, significant alternative efforts; Dishonorable Corporate Conscience Award

ADDRESS 225 East John W. Carpenter Frwy.
Irving, TX 75062-2298
L.G. Rawl, Chairman & CEO

COMPANIES	ENVIRONMENT	MINORITIES	WOMEN	DISCLOSURE
FABER/CASTELL	I	I	I	F

PRODUCTS OR SUBSIDIARIES: Eberhard Faber

ADDRESS: 4 Century Dr.
Parsippany, NJ 07054
(800) 835-8382
Christopher M. Wiedenmayer, Chairman & CEO

COMPANIES	ENVIRONMENT	MINORITIES	WOMEN	DISCLOSURE
FARAH	I	A	C	F

PRODUCTS OR SUBSIDIARIES: Farah, John Henry, Savane

ADDRESS: P.O. Box 9519
El Paso, TX 79985
Richard C. Allendar, President & CEO

COMPANIES	ENVIRONMENT	MINORITIES	WOMEN	DISCLOSURE
FARLEY INDUSTRIES	I	I	I	F

PRODUCTS OR SUBSIDIARIES: BVD, Fruit of the Loom

ADDRESS: 233 S. Wacker Dr., Suite 5000
Chicago, IL 60606
William Farley, Chairman & CEO

COMPANIES	ENVIRONMENT	MINORITIES	WOMEN	DISCLOSURE
FEDERATED DEPARTMENT STORES	A	C	C	A

PRODUCTS OR SUBSIDIARIES: Abraham & Straus, Bloomingdale's, The Bon Marche, Burdines, Jordan Marsh, Lazarus, Rich's/Goldsmith's, Stern's

ADDRESS: 7 W. 7th St.
Cincinnati, OH 45202
Allen I. Questrom, Chairman & CEO

COMPANIES	ENVIRONMENT	MINORITIES	WOMEN	DISCLOSURE
FISHER CAMUTO RETAIL	I	I	I	F
R. W. FROOKIES	I	I	I	F
THE GAP	A	I	A	F

FISHER CAMUTO RETAIL

PRODUCTS OR SUBSIDIARIES: Calico, Enzo Angiotini, Gloria Vanderbilt, Jacques Vincent, Nine West, Westies

ADDRESS: 9 W. Broad St.
Stamford, CT 06902
J. Wayne Weaver, CEO

R. W. FROOKIES

PRODUCTS OR SUBSIDIARIES: R.W. Frookies

EXTRAS: Small company

ADDRESS: P.O. Box 1649
Sag Harbor, NY 11963
Richard Worth, CEO

THE GAP

PRODUCTS OR SUBSIDIARIES: Banana Republic, The Gap

ADDRESS: 2 Harrison St.
San Francisco, CA 94105
(800) 333-7899
Donald G. Fisher, Chairman & CEO

COMPANIES	ENVIRONMENT	MINORITIES	WOMEN	DISCLOSURE
GENERAL MILLS	C	A	A	A

PRODUCTS OR SUBSIDIARIES

Basic 4, Betty Crocker, Bisquick, Body Buddies, Boo-Berry, Bugles, Buttermilk Pancake Mix, Cheerios, Cinnamon Toast Crunch, Clusters, Cocoa Puffs, Count Chocula, Country Corn Flakes, Crispy Wheats 'N Raisins, Fiber One, Franken-Berry, Fruit Roll-Ups, Fruit Shapes, Garfield Roll-Ups, Gold Medal Pouch Mixes, Golden Grahams, Granola Bars, Honey Nut Cheerios, Kaboom, Kix, Lucky Charms, Muffin Mixes, Natural Valley Granola, Nature Valley, Oatmeal Crisp, Pop Secret, Raisin Nut Bran, Robin Hood Pouch Mixes, S'Mores Grahams, Shake 'N Pour, Squeezit, Total Corn Flakes, Total Raisin Bran, Triples, Trix, Wheat Hearts, Wheat Total, Wheaties, Yoplait

EXTRAS

Corporate Conscience Awards - Charity, Equal Employment Opportunity, Opportunity for the Physically Challenged; Workplace Principles

ADDRESS

#1 General Mills Blvd.
Minneapolis, MN 55426
(800) 231-0308
H. B. Atwater, Jr., Chairman & CEO

GENESCO	C	I	F	C

PRODUCTS OR SUBSIDIARIES

C.W. Phoenix, Chaps by Ralph Lauren, Code West, Dockers shoes, Grays by Gary Wasserman, Greif, Johnston & Murphy, Kilgour French & Stanbury, Laredo, Mitre, Mondo di Marcos, Perry Ellis, Polo

ADDRESS

P.O. Box 731
Nashville, TN 37202-0731
William S. Wire, Chairman & CEO

COMPANIES	ENVIRONMENT	MINORITIES	WOMEN	DISCLOSURE
GILLETTE	C	C	C	A

PRODUCTS OR SUBSIDIARIES: Dry Idea, Jafra, Liquid Paper, Oral B, Paper Mate, Right Guard, Soft and Dri, Waterman, White Rain

EXTRAS: Animal testing: medical & non-medical purposes, significant alternative efforts

ADDRESS: Prudential Tower Building
Boston, MA 02199
Alfred M. Zeien, Chairman & CEO

COMPANIES	ENVIRONMENT	MINORITIES	WOMEN	DISCLOSURE
GITANO GROUP	A	I	I	C

PRODUCTS OR SUBSIDIARIES: Gitano

ADDRESS: 1411 Broadway
New York, NY 10018
(800) 448-2661
Morris Dabah, Chairman & CEO

COMPANIES	ENVIRONMENT	MINORITIES	WOMEN	DISCLOSURE
GRAND METROPOLITAN	C	A	C	A

PRODUCTS OR SUBSIDIARIES: Burger King, Farina, Haagen Dazs, Jeno's, Pillsbury, Totino's

EXTRAS: Factory farming; Foreign company; Teen programs & scholarships

ADDRESS: 200 South Sixth St.
Minneapolis, MN 55402
Ian A. Martin, Chairman & CEO

COMPANIES	ENVIRONMENT	MINORITIES	WOMEN	DISCLOSURE
GUESS INC.	I	I	I	F
HALLMARK CARDS	C	C	A	C
HEAD SPORTGERTE	I	I	I	F

GUESS INC.

PRODUCTS OR SUBSIDIARIES: Guess

ADDRESS: 1444 S. Alameda St.
Los Angeles, CA 90021
Georges Marciano, CEO

HALLMARK CARDS

PRODUCTS OR SUBSIDIARIES: Hallmark

EXTRAS: Corporate Conscience Award - Equal Opportunity

ADDRESS: P.O. Box 419580
Kansas City, MO 64141-6580
Irvine O. Hockaday, Jr., President & CEO

HEAD SPORTGERTE

PRODUCTS OR SUBSIDIARIES: Head Sportswear

EXTRAS: Foreign company

ADDRESS: c/o Head Sports Inc.
4801 N. 63rd St.
Boulder, CO 80301
(800) 874-3234
Bob Puccini, President

COMPANIES	ENVIRONMENT	MINORITIES	WOMEN	DISCLOSURE
HEALTH VALLEY	A	C	C	A

PRODUCTS OR SUBSIDIARIES: Amaranth Cookies, Amaranth Crunch, Apple Bakes, Corn Chips Crisp 'N Natural, Date Bakes, Fancy Fruit Chunks, Fat Free Granola Bars, Fat Free Muffins, Fat Free Organic Whole Wheat, Fat Free Sprouts 7, Fruit & Fitness, Fruit Lites, Honey Graham Crackers, No Fat Added Orangeola, Oat Bran O's, Old Fashioned Root Beer, Raisin Bakes, Stoned Wheat Crackers

ADDRESS: 16100 Foothill Blvd.
Irwindale, CA 91706
(800) 423-4846
George Mateljan, President

COMPANIES	ENVIRONMENT	MINORITIES	WOMEN	DISCLOSURE
H.J. HEINZ	A	C	C	A

PRODUCTS OR SUBSIDIARIES: Chico-San, Weight Watchers, Weight Watchers yogurt

EXTRAS: Corporate Conscience Award - Environment

ADDRESS: P.O. Box 57
Pittsburgh, PA 15230
Anthony O'Reilly, Chairman, President & CEO

COMPANIES	ENVIRONMENT	MINORITIES	WOMEN	DISCLOSURE
HELENE CURTIS	A	I	C	C

PRODUCTS OR SUBSIDIARIES: Degree, Finesse, Salon Selectives, Suave, Vibrance

EXTRAS: Animal testing: non-medical purposes

ADDRESS: 325 N. Wells St.
Chicago, IL 60610
Ronald J. Gidwitz, President & CEO

COMPANIES	ENVIRONMENT	MINORITIES	WOMEN	DISCLOSURE
HERSHEY FOODS	C	C	C	A

PRODUCTS OR SUBSIDIARIES
5th Avenue, Bar None, Hershey's, Hershey's Cocoa, Kit Kat, Krackel, Mr Goodbar, Peter Paul Almond Joy, Peter Paul Mounds, Reese's, Rolo, Skor, Special Dark, Symphony, Whatchamacallit, Y&S Twizzlers, York Peppermint Patties

EXTRAS
Animal testing: non-medical purposes, significant alternative efforts; Hershey School

ADDRESS
100 Crystal A Dr.
Hershey, PA 17033-0810
(800) 468-1714
Richard Zimmerman, Chairman & CEO

COMPANIES	ENVIRONMENT	MINORITIES	WOMEN	DISCLOSURE
HUFFY	C	F	F	A

PRODUCTS OR SUBSIDIARIES
Huffy

ADDRESS
P.O. Box 1204
Dayton, OH 45401
Harry A. Shaw III, Chairman

COMPANIES	ENVIRONMENT	MINORITIES	WOMEN	DISCLOSURE
IMASCO	I	F	C	F

PRODUCTS OR SUBSIDIARIES
Hardee's, Roy Rogers

EXTRAS
Factory farming; Fair Share; Foreign company

ADDRESS
c/o Imasco USA Inc.
1233 Hardee's Blvd.
Rocky Mount, NC 27802
Bob Autry, President

COMPANIES	ENVIRONMENT	MINORITIES	WOMEN	DISCLOSURE
INTERCO	I	I	F	F

PRODUCTS OR SUBSIDIARIES Converse, Florsheim

ADDRESS 101 S. Hanley Rd.
St. Louis, MO 63105
Richard B. Loynd, President

COMPANIES	ENVIRONMENT	MINORITIES	WOMEN	DISCLOSURE
INTERNATIONAL DAIRY QUEEN	C	F	C	A

PRODUCTS OR SUBSIDIARIES Dairy Queen, Golden Skillet, Karmelkorn, Orange Julius

ADDRESS P.O. Box 39286
Minneapolis, MN 55439-0286
Michael P. Sullivan, President & CEO

COMPANIES	ENVIRONMENT	MINORITIES	WOMEN	DISCLOSURE
J. CREW	I	I	I	F

PRODUCTS OR SUBSIDIARIES J. Crew

ADDRESS 625 Ave. of the Americas
New York, NY 10011
(800) 782-8244
Arthur Cinader, Chairman of the Board

COMPANIES	ENVIRONMENT	MINORITIES	WOMEN	DISCLOSURE
J.C. PENNEY	C	I	C	F

PRODUCTS OR SUBSIDIARIES J.C. Penney

ADDRESS 14841 N. Dallas Pkwy.
Dallas, TX 75240
William R. Howell, Chairman & CEO

COMPANIES	ENVIRONMENT	MINORITIES	WOMEN	DISCLOSURE
JOHN PAUL MITCHELL SYSTEMS	I	I	I	F

PRODUCTS OR SUBSIDIARIES: John Paul Mitchell hair care products

EXTRAS: Small company

ADDRESS: 26455 Golden Valley Rd.
Saugus, CA 91350
John Paul Jones, Chairman

COMPANIES	ENVIRONMENT	MINORITIES	WOMEN	DISCLOSURE
JOHNSON & JOHNSON	C	A	A	A

PRODUCTS OR SUBSIDIARIES: Act, Carefree, Dental Floss, Johnson's Baby Powder, Johnson's Baby Shampoo, o.b., Prevent, Reach, Shower to Shower, Stayfree, Sundown, Sure & Natural

EXTRAS: Animal testing: medical purposes only, significant alternative efforts; Direct investment in South Africa; Workplace Principles

ADDRESS: One Johnson & Johnson Plaza
New Brunswick, NJ 08933
(800) 526-3967
Ralph Larsen, Chairman & CEO

COMPANIES	ENVIRONMENT	MINORITIES	WOMEN	DISCLOSURE
S.C. JOHNSON & SON	A	C	C	A

PRODUCTS OR SUBSIDIARIES: Agree, Aveeno, Curel, Edge Gel, Halsa, Rhuli, Soft Sense Shaving Gel, Soft Sense lotion

EXTRAS: Animal testing: non-medical purposes, significant alternative efforts; Direct investment in South Africa; Workplace Principles

ADDRESS: 1525 Howe St.
Racine, WI 53403
(800) 558-5252
Richard M. Carpenter, President & CEO

COMPANIES	ENVIRONMENT	MINORITIES	WOMEN	DISCLOSURE
K-MART	C	C	A	C

PRODUCTS OR SUBSIDIARIES: K-Mart

EXTRAS: Fair Share

ADDRESS: 3100 W. Big Beaver Rd.
Troy, MI 48084
(800) 635-6278
Joseph E. Antonini, Chairman, President & CEO

COMPANIES	ENVIRONMENT	MINORITIES	WOMEN	DISCLOSURE
KELLOGG	A	A	A	A

PRODUCTS OR SUBSIDIARIES All-Bran, Apple Jacks, Apple Raisin Crisp, Bigg Mixx, Bran Buds, Bran Flakes, Cocoa Krispies, Common Sense Oat Bran, Corn Flake Crumbs, Corn Flakes, Corn Pops, Cracklin' Oat Bran, Crispix, Easy As Pie, Eggo, Frosted Flakes, Frosted Mini-Wheats, Fruit Loops, Fruitful Bran, Fruity Marshmallow Krispies, Honey Smacks, Just Right, Kenmei Rice Bran, Mrs Smith's, Mueslix, Nut & Honey Crunch, Nutri-Grain, Oatbake, Pie in Minutes, Pop Tarts, Product 19, Raisin Bran, Raisin Squares, Rice Krispies, Shredded Wheat Squares, Special K

EXTRAS Animal testing: non-medical purposes, significant alternative efforts; Corporate Conscience Awards - Employer Responsiveness, Disclosure; Direct investment in South Africa

ADDRESS P.O. Box 3599
Battle Creek, MI 49016-3599
Arnold Langbo, Chairman & CEO

COMPANIES	ENVIRONMENT	MINORITIES	WOMEN	DISCLOSURE
KIMBERLY-CLARK	F	A	A	F

PRODUCTS OR SUBSIDIARIES Chieftain, Classic, Kimberly, Kotex, Lightdays, New Freedom, Overnites, Scribe, Security, Simplique, Thin Super, Tru-Fit

EXTRAS Animal testing: non-medical purposes

ADDRESS P.O. Box 619100
Dallas, TX 75261-9100
Wayne R. Sanders, Chairman & CEO

COMPANIES	ENVIRONMENT	MINORITIES	WOMEN	DISCLOSURE
KISS MY FACE	A	C	A	A

PRODUCTS OR SUBSIDIARIES: Kiss My Face

EXTRAS: Small company

ADDRESS: P.O. Box 224
Gardiner, NY 12525
(800) 262-5477
Bob MacLeod, President

COMPANIES	ENVIRONMENT	MINORITIES	WOMEN	DISCLOSURE
LA GEAR	I	I	F	F

PRODUCTS OR SUBSIDIARIES: LA Gear

EXTRAS: Indirect ties to South Africa

ADDRESS: 4221 Redwood Ave.
Los Angeles, CA 90066
(800) 252-4327
Stanley P. Gold, Chairman & CEO

COMPANIES	ENVIRONMENT	MINORITIES	WOMEN	DISCLOSURE
LANDS'END	I	I	F	F

PRODUCTS OR SUBSIDIARIES: Lands' End backpacks, Lands' End clothing

ADDRESS: 5 Lands' End Lane
Dodgeville, WI 53595
Richard Anderson, CEO

COMPANIES	ENVIRONMENT	MINORITIES	WOMEN	DISCLOSURE
LEVI STRAUSS	C	I	A	A

PRODUCTS OR SUBSIDIARIES: Action, Brittania, Brittgear, Dockers, Levi's, Red Tab

EXTRAS: Workplace Principles

ADDRESS: 1155 Battery St.
San Francisco, CA 94111
(800) 872-5384
Robert D. Haas, Chairman & CEO

THE LIMITED	I	I	A	F

PRODUCTS OR SUBSIDIARIES: Abercrombie & Fitch, Cacique, Express, Henri Bendel, Lane Bryant, Lerner's, Limited, Penhaligon's, Structure, Victoria's Secret

ADDRESS: P.O. Box 16000
Columbus, OH 43216
Leslie H. Wexner, Chairman & President

LIZ CLAIBORNE	I	I	A	F

PRODUCTS OR SUBSIDIARIES: Dana Buchman, Elisabeth, Liz Claiborne clothing, Liz Claiborne perfume, Realities

ADDRESS: One Claiborne Ave.
North Bergen, NJ 07047
Jerome A. Chazen, Chairman & CEO

COMPANIES	ENVIRONMENT	MINORITIES	WOMEN	DISCLOSURE
LONDON INTERNATIONAL GROUP	I	I	I	F

PRODUCTS OR SUBSIDIARIES: Durex, Excita, Fourex, Koromex, Protex, Ramses, Sheik

EXTRAS: Foreign company

ADDRESS: 1819 Main St.
Sarasota, FL 34236
Kenneth Matthews, President

COMPANIES	ENVIRONMENT	MINORITIES	WOMEN	DISCLOSURE
L'OREAL	C	C	A	A

PRODUCTS OR SUBSIDIARIES: Anais Anais, Biotherm, Cacharel, Giorgio Armani, Gloria Vanderbilt, Guy Laroche, L'Oreal makeup, L'Oreal shampoo, L'Oreal skin care, Lancome, Paloma Picasso, Ralph Lauren perfume

EXTRAS: Animal testing: non-medical purposes, significant alternative efforts; Foreign company

ADDRESS: c/o Cosmair Inc.
575 Fifth Ave.
New York, NY 10017
(800) 631-7358
Guy Perelongue, President & CEO

COMPANIES	ENVIRONMENT	MINORITIES	WOMEN	DISCLOSURE
LOST ARROW	A	F	A	A

PRODUCTS OR SUBSIDIARIES: Patagonia

ADDRESS: P.O. Box 150
Ventura, CA 93002
(800) 523-9597
Yvon Chouinard, Chairman

COMPANIES	ENVIRONMENT	MINORITIES	WOMEN	DISCLOSURE
R.H. MACY	I	I	I	F

PRODUCTS OR SUBSIDIARIES: Bullock's, I. Magnin, Macy's

EXTRAS: Workplace Principles

ADDRESS: 151 W. 34th St.
New York, NY 10001
(800) 743-6229
Mark S. Handler, Chairman & CEO

COMPANIES	ENVIRONMENT	MINORITIES	WOMEN	DISCLOSURE
MARS	C	I	A	A

PRODUCTS OR SUBSIDIARIES: 3 Musketeers, Combos, Dove, Kudos, M & M's, Mars, Milky Way, Rondos, Skittles, Snickers, Starburst, Summit, Twix

ADDRESS: 6885 Elm St.
Mc Lean, VA 22101
Forrest E. Mars, Co-President

COMPANIES	ENVIRONMENT	MINORITIES	WOMEN	DISCLOSURE
MATRIX ESSENTIALS	I	I	I	F

PRODUCTS OR SUBSIDIARIES: Matrix

ADDRESS: 30601 Carter St.
Solon, OH 44139
(800) 282-2822
Bob Evans, CFO

COMPANIES	ENVIRONMENT	MINORITIES	WOMEN	DISCLOSURE
MATSUSHITA ELECTRIC INDUSTRIAL	C	I	I	F

PRODUCTS OR SUBSIDIARIES DGC Records, Geffen Records, MCA Records

EXTRAS Fair Share; Foreign company

ADDRESS c/o Matsushita Elec. Co. of America
One Panasonic Way
Secaucus, NJ 07094
Akiya Imura, Chairman & CEO

COMPANIES	ENVIRONMENT	MINORITIES	WOMEN	DISCLOSURE
MAY DEPARTMENT STORES	I	C	A	A

PRODUCTS OR SUBSIDIARIES Filene's, Foley's, Lord & Taylor, PayLess Shoe Source

EXTRAS Workplace Principles

ADDRESS 611 Olive St.
St Louis, MO 63101
David C. Farrell, Chairman & CEO

COMPANIES	ENVIRONMENT	MINORITIES	WOMEN	DISCLOSURE
MCDONALD'S	C	A	C	C

PRODUCTS OR SUBSIDIARIES McDonald's

EXTRAS Factory farming; Fair Share; Teen programs & scholarships

ADDRESS 1 Campus Office Bldg. Kroc Dr.
Oak Brook, IL 60521
Michael R. Quinlan, Chairman & CEO

COMPANIES	ENVIRONMENT	MINORITIES	WOMEN	DISCLOSURE
MEAD	F	C	C	C

PRODUCTS OR SUBSIDIARIES: Mead

EXTRAS: Workplace Principles

ADDRESS: Courthouse Plaza NE
Dayton, OH 45463
Steven C. Mason, Chairman & CEO

COMPANIES	ENVIRONMENT	MINORITIES	WOMEN	DISCLOSURE
MEM CO.	I	I	A	C

PRODUCTS OR SUBSIDIARIES: English Leather, Fathom, Heaven Sent, Love's

ADDRESS: P.O. Box 928
Northvale, NJ 07647
Gay A. Mayer, Chairman, President & CEO

COMPANIES	ENVIRONMENT	MINORITIES	WOMEN	DISCLOSURE
MINN. MINING & MFG. (3M)	C	A	A	A

PRODUCTS OR SUBSIDIARIES: Buf Puf, Post-It, Scotch

EXTRAS: Animal testing: medical & non-medical purposes; Direct investment in South Africa

ADDRESS: 3M Center
St. Paul, MN 55144-1000
Libio Desimone, Chairman & CEO

COMPANIES	ENVIRONMENT	MINORITIES	WOMEN	DISCLOSURE
MOBIL	F	C	C	A

PRODUCTS OR SUBSIDIARIES — Mobil

EXTRAS — Animal testing: non-medical purposes, significant alternative efforts; Workplace Principles

ADDRESS — 3225 Gallows Rd.
Fairfax, VA 22037-0001
Allen E. Murray, Chairman & CEO

COMPANIES	ENVIRONMENT	MINORITIES	WOMEN	DISCLOSURE
NA NA TRADING CO.	A	F	A	A

PRODUCTS OR SUBSIDIARIES — Doc Martens, Na Na clothing, Na Na shoes, Utility, Weltware

EXTRAS — Small company

ADDRESS — 1228 3rd St.
Santa Monica, CA 90401
Paul Kaufman, Co-Owner

COMPANIES	ENVIRONMENT	MINORITIES	WOMEN	DISCLOSURE
NESTLE	C	I	C	A

PRODUCTS OR SUBSIDIARIES — After Eight Dinner Mints, Baby Ruth, Bon Bons, Butterfinger, Carnation, Chunky, Goobers, Libby, Nestea, Nestle, Nestle Cocoa, Oh Henry!, Perrier, Quik, Raisinets, Sno-Caps

EXTRAS — Animal testing: non-medical purposes, significant alternative efforts; Direct investment in South Africa; Foreign company; Infant formula

ADDRESS — 800 N. Brand Blvd.
Glendale, CA 91203
Timm F. Crull, Chairman & CEO

COMPANIES	ENVIRONMENT	MINORITIES	WOMEN	DISCLOSURE
NEUTROGENA	A	I	C	F

PRODUCTS OR SUBSIDIARIES: Neutrogena hair care, Neutrogena skin care

ADDRESS: 5760 W. 96th St.
Los Angeles, CA 90045
(800) 421-6857
Lloyd E. Cotsen, President & CEO

COMPANIES	ENVIRONMENT	MINORITIES	WOMEN	DISCLOSURE
NEW BALANCE	I	I	I	F

PRODUCTS OR SUBSIDIARIES: New Balance

ADDRESS: 38-42 Everett St.
Boston, MA 02134
(800) 343-1395
James S. Davis, Chairman

COMPANIES	ENVIRONMENT	MINORITIES	WOMEN	DISCLOSURE
NEWMAN'S OWN	A	C	A	A

PRODUCTS OR SUBSIDIARIES: Newman's lemonade, Newman's popcorn

EXTRAS: 100% profit to charity; Corporate Conscience Award - Charity; Small company

ADDRESS: 246 Post Rd. East
Westport, CT 06880
Paul Newman, President

COMPANIES	ENVIRONMENT	MINORITIES	WOMEN	DISCLOSURE
NEXXUS PRODUCTS	I	I	I	F

PRODUCTS OR SUBSIDIARIES: Nexxus

EXTRAS: Small company

ADDRESS: P.O. Box 1274
Santa Barbara, CA 93116
Jheri Redding, CEO

COMPANIES	ENVIRONMENT	MINORITIES	WOMEN	DISCLOSURE
NIKE	C	F	C	A

PRODUCTS OR SUBSIDIARIES: Cole Haan, Nike clothing, Nike shoes, Nike stores

ADDRESS: One Bowerman Dr.
Beaverton, OR 97005-6453
(800) 344-6453
Philip H. Knight, Chairman & CEO

COMPANIES	ENVIRONMENT	MINORITIES	WOMEN	DISCLOSURE
NORDSTROM	A	A	A	A

PRODUCTS OR SUBSIDIARIES: Nordstrom

ADDRESS: 1501 Fifth Ave.
Seattle, WA 98101-1603
Bruce Nordstrom, Co-Chair

COMPANIES	ENVIRONMENT	MINORITIES	WOMEN	DISCLOSURE
OCEAN PACIFIC SUNWEAR	I	I	I	F
ORJENE NATURAL COSMETICS	A	A	A	A
PACIFIC DUNLOP HOLDING	I	I	I	F

OCEAN PACIFIC SUNWEAR

PRODUCTS OR SUBSIDIARIES: Ocean Pacific

EXTRAS: Small company

ADDRESS: 2701 Dow Ave.
Tustin, CA 92680
(800) 899-6775
James Jenks, CEO

ORJENE NATURAL COSMETICS

PRODUCTS OR SUBSIDIARIES: Avocado Oils, Orjene Natural Cosmetics, Vit-A-Skin Cream

EXTRAS: Small company

ADDRESS: 5-43 48th Ave.
Long Island City, NY 11101
(800) 886-7536
Dennis Machicao, CEO

PACIFIC DUNLOP HOLDING

PRODUCTS OR SUBSIDIARIES: Lifestyles

EXTRAS: Foreign company

ADDRESS: 10 S. La Salle St., Ste. 3712
Chicago, IL 60603
Ian Veal, President

COMPANIES	ENVIRONMENT	MINORITIES	WOMEN	DISCLOSURE
PEPSICO	C	A	A	A

PRODUCTS OR SUBSIDIARIES: 7-UP, Chee-tos, Delta Gold, Doritos, Fritos, Fun-Yuns, Grandma's, Kentucky Fried Chicken, Lay's, Mountain Dew, Mug, Munchos, O'Grady's, Pepsi Cola, Pizza Hut, Rold Gold, Ruffles, Salsa Rio, Slice, Smartfood, Taco Bell, Tostitos

EXTRAS: Animal testing: non-medical purposes; Factory farming; Indirect ties to South Africa; Teen programs & scholarships

ADDRESS: 700 Anderson Hill Rd.
Purchase, NY 10577-1444
D. Wayne Calloway, Chairman & CEO

COMPANIES	ENVIRONMENT	MINORITIES	WOMEN	DISCLOSURE
PET INC.	I	I	C	F

PRODUCTS OR SUBSIDIARIES: Downyflake, Whitman's Chocolates

ADDRESS: 400 South Fourth St.
St. Louis, MO 63102
Miles Marsh, CEO

COMPANIES	ENVIRONMENT	MINORITIES	WOMEN	DISCLOSURE
PFIZER	F	I	C	F

PRODUCTS OR SUBSIDIARIES: Barbasol, Essence mousse, Exclamation, Iron cologne, L'Effleur, Lady Stetson, Musk for Men, Plax mouthwash, Preferred Stock, Sophia perfume, Stetson

EXTRAS: Animal testing: medical purposes only; Direct investment in South Africa; Workplace Principles

ADDRESS: 235 East 42nd St.
New York, NY 10017
W.C. Steere, Chairman & CEO

COMPANIES	ENVIRONMENT	MINORITIES	WOMEN	DISCLOSURE
PHILIP MORRIS	F	A	A	F

PRODUCTS OR SUBSIDIARIES: Breyer's, Country Time, Crystal Light, Frosted Rice Krinkles, Fruit & Fibre, Frusen Gladje, Grape-Nuts, Honey Bunches of Oats, Honey Nut Crunch, Honeycomb, Kool-Aid, Light n' Lively, Post Grape Nuts, Post Raisin Bran, Tang, Toblerone, Wyler's

EXTRAS: Animal testing: non-medical purposes; Cigarettes; Indirect ties to South Africa; Workplace Principles

ADDRESS: 120 Park Ave.
New York, NY 10017
Michael Miles, Chairman & CEO

COMPANIES	ENVIRONMENT	MINORITIES	WOMEN	DISCLOSURE
PHILIPS' GLOEILAMPEN-FABRIEKEN	I	I	I	F

PRODUCTS OR SUBSIDIARIES: Mercury, Polygram Records

EXTRAS: Foreign company

ADDRESS: 100 E. 42nd St.
New York, NY 10017
Stephen C. Tumminello, President & CEO

COMPANIES	ENVIRONMENT	MINORITIES	WOMEN	DISCLOSURE
PHILLIPS PETROLEUM	F	C	C	A

PRODUCTS OR SUBSIDIARIES: Phillips 66

ADDRESS: 18 Phillips Building
Bartlesville, OK 74004
C. J. Silas, President & CEO

COMPANIES	ENVIRONMENT	MINORITIES	WOMEN	DISCLOSURE

PHILLIPS-VAN HEUSEN	I	I	C	F

PRODUCTS OR SUBSIDIARIES: Phillips-Van Heusen

ADDRESS: 1290 Ave. of the Americas
New York, NY 10104
(800) 777-1726
Lawrence S. Phillips, Chairman & CEO

PLAYTEX FP GROUP	I	I	I	F

PRODUCTS OR SUBSIDIARIES: Jhirmack, Playtex, Tek, Ultimates

EXTRAS: Animal testing: non-medical purposes

ADDRESS: P.O. Box 10064
Stamford, CT 06904
Joel E. Smilow, Chairman & CEO

PRINCE MANUFACTURING	I	I	I	F

PRODUCTS OR SUBSIDIARIES: Prince

ADDRESS: P.O. Box 2031
Princeton, NJ 08543-2031
(800) 283-6647
John Sullivan, Chairman

COMPANIES	ENVIRONMENT	MINORITIES	WOMEN	DISCLOSURE
PROCTER & GAMBLE	C	A	C	A

PRODUCTS OR SUBSIDIARIES
Always, Bain de Soleil, California, Camay, Clarion, Clearasil, Coast, Cover Girl, Crest, Denquel, Fisher Nuts, Gleem, Hawaiian Punch, Head & Shoulders, Hugo Boss, Ivory shampoo, Ivory soap, Kirk's, Laura Biagiotti-Romst, le Jardin, Lincoln, Max Factor, Navy by Cover Girl, Noxzema, Oil of Olay, Old Spice, Pantene, Pert Plus, Prell, Pringles, Rain Tree, Safeguard, Scope, Secret, Sunny Delight, Sure, Texsun, Toujours Moi, Vidal Sassoon, Wondra, Zest

EXTRAS
Animal testing: medical and non-medical purposes, significant alternative efforts; Corporate Conscience Awards - Animal Welfare, Employer Responsiveness; Indirect ties to South Africa; Workplace Principles

ADDRESS
P.O. Box 599
Cincinnati, OH 45201
Edwin Artzt, Chairman & CEO

COMPANIES	ENVIRONMENT	MINORITIES	WOMEN	DISCLOSURE
QUAKER OATS	C	A	A	A

PRODUCTS OR SUBSIDIARIES
Aunt Jemima pancake mixes and syrup, Cap'n Crunch, Celeste Pizza, Gatorade, Granola Dipps, Life, Oh's, Quaker 100% Natural cereal, Quaker Oat Squares, Quaker Oatmeal, Rice Cakes, Van Camp's products, Whipps

EXTRAS
Fair Share

ADDRESS
321 N. Clark St.
Chicago, IL 60610
William D. Smithburg, Chairman & CEO

COMPANIES	ENVIRONMENT	MINORITIES	WOMEN	DISCLOSURE
RJR NABISCO	F	I	C	F

PRODUCTS OR SUBSIDIARIES: Almost Home, Barnum's Animals, Better Cheddars, Breathsavers, Bubble Yum, Carefree, Chips Ahoy, Cream of Wheat, Fig Newtons, Honey Maid, Lifesavers, Mallomars, Nabisco Raisin Bran, Newtons, Oreos, Planters, Premium, Ritz, Shredded Wheat, Triscuit, Wheat Thins

EXTRAS: Animal testing: non-medical purposes; Cigarettes; Dishonorable Corporate Conscience Award; Workplace Principles

ADDRESS: 1301 Ave. of the Americas
New York, NY 10019
Louis Gerstner, CEO

COMPANIES	ENVIRONMENT	MINORITIES	WOMEN	DISCLOSURE
RACHEL PERRY	A	A	A	A

PRODUCTS OR SUBSIDIARIES: Rachel Perry

EXTRAS: Small company

ADDRESS: 9111 Mason Ave.
Chatsworth, CA 91311
(800) 966-8888
David Hu, Controller

COMPANIES	ENVIRONMENT	MINORITIES	WOMEN	DISCLOSURE
RALSTON PURINA	F	A	C	A

PRODUCTS OR SUBSIDIARIES — Chex, Cookie Crisp, Hostess, Muesli, Ry Krisp, Teenage Mutant Ninja Turtles

ADDRESS — Checkerboard Square
St. Louis, MO 63164
William P. Stiritz, Chairman & CEO

COMPANIES	ENVIRONMENT	MINORITIES	WOMEN	DISCLOSURE
RECKITT & COLMAN	I	I	I	F

PRODUCTS OR SUBSIDIARIES — Binaca, Durkee's, Neet

EXTRA — Animal testing: non-medical purposes; Foreign company

ADDRESS — 1655 Valley Rd.
Wayne, NJ 07470

COMPANIES	ENVIRONMENT	MINORITIES	WOMEN	DISCLOSURE
REDKEN LABORATORIES	A	I	A	C

PRODUCTS OR SUBSIDIARIES — Intervals, Redken shampoo, Redken skin care

ADDRESS — 6625 Variel Ave.
Canoga Park, CA 91303
(800) 423-5369
Paula K. Meehan, Chairman

COMPANIES	ENVIRONMENT	MINORITIES	WOMEN	DISCLOSURE
REEBOK INTERNATIONAL	C	I	F	F

PRODUCTS OR SUBSIDIARIES: Avia, Ellesse, Reebok clothing, Reebok shoes, Rockport

ADDRESS: 100 Technology Center Dr.
Stoughton, MA 02072
(800) 843-4444
Paul Fireman, Chairman & CEO

COMPANIES	ENVIRONMENT	MINORITIES	WOMEN	DISCLOSURE
REVLON	C	I	I	F

PRODUCTS OR SUBSIDIARIES: Alexandra de Markoff, Almay, Bill Blass, Charles of the Ritz, Halston, New Essentials, Revlon, Roux, Ultima II

ADDRESS: 625 Madison Ave.
New York, NY 10022
(800) 334-8332
Ronald Perelman, Chairman & CEO

COMPANIES	ENVIRONMENT	MINORITIES	WOMEN	DISCLOSURE
RHINO RECORDS	A	A	A	A

PRODUCTS OR SUBSIDIARIES: Rhino Records

EXTRAS: Small company

ADDRESS: 2225 Colorado Ave.
Santa Monica, CA 90404
Richard Foos, President

COMPANIES	ENVIRONMENT	MINORITIES	WOMEN	DISCLOSURE
ROYAL DUTCH/SHELL	C	C	F	A

PRODUCTS OR SUBSIDIARIES: Shell

EXTRAS: Animal testing: non-medical purposes, significant alternative efforts; Direct investment in South Africa; Foreign company

ADDRESS: c/o Shell Oil Company, USA
One Shell Plaza
Houston, TX 77252
Frank H. Richardson, President

COMPANIES	ENVIRONMENT	MINORITIES	WOMEN	DISCLOSURE
RUSSELL	C	I	F	F

PRODUCTS OR SUBSIDIARIES: Jerzees, Russell Athletic

ADDRESS: P.O. Box 272
Alexander City, AL 35010
Eugene C. Gwaltney, CEO

COMPANIES	ENVIRONMENT	MINORITIES	WOMEN	DISCLOSURE
SAM & LIBBY	I	I	I	F

PRODUCTS OR SUBSIDIARIES: Sam & Libby

EXTRAS: Small company

ADDRESS: 1123 Industrial Rd.
San Carlos, CA 94070
Samuel L. Edelman, President & CEO

COMPANIES	ENVIRONMENT	MINORITIES	WOMEN	DISCLOSURE
SANFORD	A	I	I	F

PRODUCTS OR SUBSIDIARIES: Accent, Sanford

ADDRESS: 2711 Washington Blvd.
Bellwood, IL 60104
Henry B. Pearsall, Chairman & CEO

COMPANIES	ENVIRONMENT	MINORITIES	WOMEN	DISCLOSURE
SARA LEE	C	C	A	A

PRODUCTS OR SUBSIDIARIES: Champion, Dim hosiery, Donna Karan hosiery, Hanes, Isotoner, L'Eggs, Liz Claiborne hosiery, Playtex, Pretty Polly hosiery, Sara Lee desserts

EXTRAS: Corporate Conscience Award - Charity; Indirect ties to South Africa

ADDRESS: Three First National Plaza
Chicago, IL 60602-4260
John H. Bryan, Jr., Chairman & CEO

COMPANIES	ENVIRONMENT	MINORITIES	WOMEN	DISCLOSURE
SASSON LICENSING	I	I	I	F

PRODUCTS OR SUBSIDIARIES: Sasson jeans

ADDRESS: 1133 Ave. of the Americas
New York, NY 10036
Bob Lankenau, CFO

COMPANIES	ENVIRONMENT	MINORITIES	WOMEN	DISCLOSURE
SCHERING-PLOUGH	C	A	C	A

PRODUCTS OR SUBSIDIARIES — A & D Ointment, Complex 15, Coppertone, Shade, Solarcaine, Tropical Blend, Zinka

EXTRAS — Animal testing: medical & non-medical purposes, significant alternative efforts; Direct investment in South Africa; Workplace Principles

ADDRESS — One Giralda Farms
Madison, NJ 07940-1000
Robert P. Luciano, Chairman & CEO

COMPANIES	ENVIRONMENT	MINORITIES	WOMEN	DISCLOSURE
SEARS, ROEBUCK	C	C	C	A

PRODUCTS OR SUBSIDIARIES — Sears

ADDRESS — Sears Tower
Chicago, IL 60684
Edward A. Brennan, Chairman & CEO

COMPANIES	ENVIRONMENT	MINORITIES	WOMEN	DISCLOSURE
SEBASTIAN INTERNATIONAL	A	I	I	F

PRODUCTS OR SUBSIDIARIES — Sebastian

ADDRESS — 6109 DeSoto Ave.
Woodland Hills, CA 91367
(800) 829-7322
John Sebastian, Chairman & President

COMPANIES	ENVIRONMENT	MINORITIES	WOMEN	DISCLOSURE
SEVENTH GENERATION	A	C	A	A

PRODUCTS OR SUBSIDIARIES: Rainforest Crisp, Rainforest Crunch, Seventh Generation clothing, Seventh Generation sanitary pads, Seventh Generation skin care

EXTRAS: CERES Principles; Small company

ADDRESS: 49 Hercules Dr.
Colchester, VT 05446-1672
(800) 456-1177
Jeffrey Hollender, President & CEO

COMPANIES	ENVIRONMENT	MINORITIES	WOMEN	DISCLOSURE
SHISEIDO	I	I	C	F

PRODUCTS OR SUBSIDIARIES: Shiseido

EXTRAS: Animal testing: non-medical purposes; Foreign company

ADDRESS: c/o Shiseido Cosmetics America Ltd.
900 Third Ave., 15th fl.
New York, NY 10022
(800) 223-0424
Sadao Abe, President & CEO

COMPANIES	ENVIRONMENT	MINORITIES	WOMEN	DISCLOSURE
SMITHKLINE BEECHAM	C	C	C	A

PRODUCTS OR SUBSIDIARIES: Oxy

EXTRAS: Animal testing: medical purposes only, significant alternative efforts; Foreign company; Workplace Principles

ADDRESS: One Franklin Plaza
Philadelphia, PA 19102-1225
Robert Bauman, CEO

COMPANIES	ENVIRONMENT	MINORITIES	WOMEN	DISCLOSURE
SONY	A	A	C	A

PRODUCTS OR SUBSIDIARIES: Columbia Records, Epic Records

EXTRAS: Fair Share; Foreign company; Teen programs & scholarships

ADDRESS: c/o Sony Corp of America
One Sony Dr.
Park Ridge, NJ 07656
K. Iwaki, Chairman & CEO

COMPANIES	ENVIRONMENT	MINORITIES	WOMEN	DISCLOSURE
SPALDING & EVENFLO	I	I	I	F

PRODUCTS OR SUBSIDIARIES: Spalding

ADDRESS: P.O. Box 30101
Tampa, FL 33630
Donald Byrnes, President & CEO

COMPANIES	ENVIRONMENT	MINORITIES	WOMEN	DISCLOSURE
STONYFIELD FARM	A	C	A	A

PRODUCTS OR SUBSIDIARIES: Stonyfield Farm

EXTRAS: CERES Principles; Small company

ADDRESS: 10 Burton Dr.
Londonderry, NH 03053
Gary Hirshberg, CEO

COMPANIES	ENVIRONMENT	MINORITIES	WOMEN	DISCLOSURE
STRIDE-RITE	C	I	A	C

PRODUCTS OR SUBSIDIARIES: Keds, Sperry Top-Sider, Stride-Rite

EXTRAS: Teen programs & scholarships

ADDRESS: 5 Cambridge Center
Cambridge, MA 02142
Ervin R. Shames, Chairman & CEO

COMPANIES	ENVIRONMENT	MINORITIES	WOMEN	DISCLOSURE
SUN COMPANY	F	I	F	F

PRODUCTS OR SUBSIDIARIES: Sunoco

ADDRESS: 10 Penn Center
Radnor, PA 19103
Robert McClements, Jr., Chairman

COMPANIES	ENVIRONMENT	MINORITIES	WOMEN	DISCLOSURE
SUNSHINE BISCUITS	I	I	I	F

PRODUCTS OR SUBSIDIARIES: Bavarian Fingers, Cheez-It, Chip-A-Roos, Country Styles, Doubles, Hydrox, Vienna Fingers

ADDRESS: 100 Woodbridge Center Dr.
Woodbridge, NJ 07095
(800) 242-7449
Wilfred Uytengsu, CEO

COMPANIES	ENVIRONMENT	MINORITIES	WOMEN	DISCLOSURE
TAMBRANDS	A	I	C	C

PRODUCTS OR SUBSIDIARIES: Tampax

EXTRAS: Indirect ties to South Africa

ADDRESS: 777 Westchester Ave.
White Plains, NY 10604
(800) 523-0014
Martin F. Emmett, Chairman & CEO

COMPANIES	ENVIRONMENT	MINORITIES	WOMEN	DISCLOSURE
TEXACO	F	F	F	A

PRODUCTS OR SUBSIDIARIES: Texaco

EXTRAS: Animal testing: non-medical purposes; Direct investment in South Africa

ADDRESS: 2000 Westchester Ave.
White Plains, NY 10650
James W. Kinnean, President & CEO

COMPANIES	ENVIRONMENT	MINORITIES	WOMEN	DISCLOSURE
THORN EMI	I	I	I	C

PRODUCTS OR SUBSIDIARIES: Capitol Records, Chrysalis Records, EMI Records, SBK Records

EXTRAS: Foreign Company; Nuclear weapons

ADDRESS: c/o EMI Music Worldwide
152 W. 57th St.
New York, NY 10019
Charles Koppleman, President

COMPANIES	ENVIRONMENT	MINORITIES	WOMEN	DISCLOSURE
TIMBERLAND	A	F	C	A

PRODUCTS OR SUBSIDIARIES: Timberland clothes, Timberland shoes, Timberland stores

ADDRESS: P.O. Box 5050
Hampton, NH 03842
(800) 258-0855
Sidney W. Swartz, Chairman, President & CEO

COMPANIES	ENVIRONMENT	MINORITIES	WOMEN	DISCLOSURE
TIME WARNER	C	A	A	A

PRODUCTS OR SUBSIDIARIES — Atlantic Records, Elektra Records, Warner Bros. Records

EXTRAS — Indirect ties to South Africa; Teen programs & scholarships; Workplace Principles

ADDRESS — 75 Rockefeller Plaza
New York, NY 10019
Steven J. Ross, Chairman

COMPANIES	ENVIRONMENT	MINORITIES	WOMEN	DISCLOSURE
TOM'S OF MAINE	A	C	A	A

PRODUCTS OR SUBSIDIARIES — Tom's of Maine

EXTRAS — CERES Principles; Corporate Conscience Award - Charity; Small company

ADDRESS — P. O. Box 710
Kennebunk, ME 04043
(800) 367-8667
Tom Chappell, President

COMPANIES	ENVIRONMENT	MINORITIES	WOMEN	DISCLOSURE
TOPPS CHEWING GUM	I	I	F	F

PRODUCTS OR SUBSIDIARIES — Bazooka, Hockey, Ring Pop, Sundae Cone Candy, Topps, Zooks

ADDRESS — 254-36th St.
Brooklyn, NY 11232
Arthur T. Shorin, Chairman & CEO

COMPANIES	ENVIRONMENT	MINORITIES	WOMEN	DISCLOSURE
US SHOE	I	I	F	F

PRODUCTS OR SUBSIDIARIES
Antics, Capezio, Casual Corner, Cobbies, Eastwood Place, Easy Spirit, Joyce, L-S-P, Pappagallo, Selby, Ups 'N Downs

ADDRESS
1 Eastwood Dr.
Cincinnati, OH 45227
Bannus Hudson, CEO

COMPANIES	ENVIRONMENT	MINORITIES	WOMEN	DISCLOSURE
USX CORP.	F	F	F	F

PRODUCTS OR SUBSIDIARIES
Marathon

EXTRAS
Dishonorable Corporate Conscience Award; Indirect ties to South Africa

ADDRESS
600 Grant St.
Pittsburgh, PA 15219
Charles A. Corry, Chairman & CEO

COMPANIES	ENVIRONMENT	MINORITIES	WOMEN	DISCLOSURE
UNILEVER	C	F	F	A

PRODUCTS OR SUBSIDIARIES
Aim, Aqua Net, Brut 33, Calvin Klein, Caress, Close-Up, Cutex, Dove, Elizabeth Arden makeup, Elizabeth Arden perfume, Eternity, Faberge, Good Humor, Lux, Magnum, Obsession, Pond's, Popsicle, Shield, Signal, Sky, Timotei, Vaseline, Wyler's

EXTRAS
Animal testing: non-medical purposes, significant alternative efforts; Foreign company

ADDRESS
390 Park Ave.
New York, NY 10022
(800) 451-6679
Richard A. Goldstein, CEO

COMPANIES	ENVIRONMENT	MINORITIES	WOMEN	DISCLOSURE
UNITED BISCUITS	A	F	F	F

PRODUCTS OR SUBSIDIARIES: Chips Deluxe, Elfkins, Hooplas, Keebler, Keebler Soft Batch, Munch'ems, O'Boisies, Pecan Sandies, Pizzarias, Ripplin's, Town House, Wheatables, Zesta

EXTRAS: Foreign company

ADDRESS: c/o Keebler Company
One Hollow Tree Lane
Elmhurst, IL 60126
Thomas M. Garvin, President & CEO

COMPANIES	ENVIRONMENT	MINORITIES	WOMEN	DISCLOSURE
V.F. CORP.	C	I	C	F

PRODUCTS OR SUBSIDIARIES: Barbizon, Basset Walker, Bolero, JanSport, Jantzen, Lee, Lollipop, Marithe Francois Girbaud, O Wear, Rustler, Silhouette, Siltex, Vanity Fair, Variance, Vassarette, Wrangler

ADDRESS: 1047 N. Park Rd.
Wyomissing, PA 19610
Lawrence Pugh, CEO

COMPANIES	ENVIRONMENT	MINORITIES	WOMEN	DISCLOSURE
WAL-MART STORES	A	I	I	F

PRODUCTS OR SUBSIDIARIES: Sam's Club, Wal-Mart

ADDRESS: 702 S.W. 8th St.
Bentonville, AR 72716
David Glass, President & CEO

COMPANIES	ENVIRONMENT	MINORITIES	WOMEN	DISCLOSURE
WARNER-LAMBERT	C	A	C	A

PRODUCTS OR SUBSIDIARIES: Bubblicious, Certs, Charleston Chew!, Chewels, Chiclets, Clorets, Dentyne, Freshen-Up, Junior Mints, Listermint, Personal Touch, Pom Poms, Schick, Sticklets, Sugar Babies, Sugar Daddy, Trident

EXTRAS: Animal testing: medical purposes only; Direct investment in South Africa; Workplace Principles

ADDRESS: 201 Tabor Rd.
Morris Plains, NJ 07950
Melvin R. Goodes, Chairman & CEO

COMPANIES	ENVIRONMENT	MINORITIES	WOMEN	DISCLOSURE
WEETABIX	I	I	I	F

PRODUCTS OR SUBSIDIARIES: Grainfields

EXTRAS: Foreign company

ADDRESS: 20 Cameron St .
Clinton, MA 01510
(800) 343-0590
John H. Carver, President

COMPANIES	ENVIRONMENT	MINORITIES	WOMEN	DISCLOSURE
WENDY'S INTERNATIONAL	A	I	A	C

PRODUCTS OR SUBSIDIARIES: Wendy's

EXTRAS: Factory farming; Fair Share

ADDRESS: P.O. Box 256
Dublin, OH 43017
James W. Near, Chairman & CEO

COMPANIES	ENVIRONMENT	MINORITIES	WOMEN	DISCLOSURE
WOLVERINE WORLD WIDE	I	I	C	F

PRODUCTS OR SUBSIDIARIES: Bates Floaters, Brooks, Coleman, Hush Puppies, Sioux Mox, Town & Country, Tru-Stitch, Wilderness, Wimzees, Wolverine

ADDRESS: 9341 Courtland Dr.
Rockford, MI 49351
Thomas D. Gleason, Chairman & CEO

COMPANIES	ENVIRONMENT	MINORITIES	WOMEN	DISCLOSURE
WM. WRIGLEY JR.	C	I	F	F

PRODUCTS OR SUBSIDIARIES: Big League Chew, Big Red, Bubble Tape, Doublemint, Extra Sugarfree Gum, Freedent, Hubba Bubba, Juicy Fruit, Reed Candy Company, Winter Fresh, Wrigley's

EXTRAS: Fair Share

ADDRESS: 410 N. Michigan Ave.
Chicago, IL 60611
(800) 824-9687
William Wrigley, President & CEO

CHAPTER 9

Shopping for your future

Ratings by Product

COMPANIES	ENVIRONMENT	MINORITIES	WOMEN	DISCLOSURE
AMERICAN HOME PRODUCTS	F	F	C	A

PRODUCTS OR SUBSIDIARIES: Maypo Oatmeal, Wheatena

EXTRAS: Animal testing: medical & non-medical purposes, significant alternative efforts; Infant formula; Indirect ties to South Africa

COMPANIES	ENVIRONMENT	MINORITIES	WOMEN	DISCLOSURE
BORDEN	F	A	C	A

PRODUCTS OR SUBSIDIARIES: Cary's, Lite-line, MacDonald's, Mountain High, Vermont Maple Or., Viva yogurt

EXTRAS: Direct investment in South Africa

COMPANIES	ENVIRONMENT	MINORITIES	WOMEN	DISCLOSURE
GENERAL MILLS	C	A	A	A

PRODUCTS OR SUBSIDIARIES: Basic 4, Betty Crocker, Bisquick, Boo-Berry, Buttermilk Pancake Mix, Cheerios, Cinnamon Toast Crunch, Clusters, Cocoa Puffs, Count Chocula, Country Corn Flakes, Crispy Wheats 'N Raisins, Fiber One, Franken-Berry, Gold Medal Pouch Mixes, Golden Grahams, Honey Nut Cheerios, Kaboom, Kix, Lucky Charms, Natural Valley Granola, Oatmeal Crisp, Raisin Nut Bran, Robin Hood Pouch Mixes, S'Mores Grahams, Shake 'N Pour, Total Corn Flakes, Total Raisin Bran, Triples, Trix, Wheat Hearts, Wheat Total, Wheaties, Yoplait

EXTRAS: Corporate Conscience Awards - Charity, Equal Employment Opportunity, Opportunity for the Physically Challenged; Workplace Principles

COMPANIES	ENVIRONMENT	MINORITIES	WOMEN	DISCLOSURE
GRAND METROPOLITAN	C	A	C	A
PRODUCTS OR SUBSIDIARIES	Farina			
EXTRAS	Factory farming; Foreign company; Teen programs & scholarships			
HEALTH VALLEY	A	C	C	A
PRODUCTS OR SUBSIDIARIES	Amaranth Crunch, Fat Free Sprouts 7, Fruit & Fitness, Fruit Lites, No Fat Added Orangeola, Oat Bran O's			
H.J. HEINZ	A	C	C	A
PRODUCTS OR SUBSIDIARIES	Weight Watchers yogurt			
EXTRAS	Corporate Conscience Award - Environment			
KELLOGG	A	A	A	A
PRODUCTS OR SUBSIDIARIES	All-Bran, Apple Jacks, Apple Raisin Crisp, Bigg Mixx, Bran Buds, Bran Flakes, Cocoa Krispies, Common Sense Oat Bran, Corn Flake Crumbs, Corn Flakes, Corn Pops, Cracklin' Oat Bran, Crispix, Eggo, Frosted Flakes, Frosted Mini-Wheats, Fruit Loops, Fruitful Bran, Fruity Marshmallow Krispies, Honey Smacks, Just Right, Kenmei Rice Bran, Mueslix, Nut & Honey Crunch, Nutri-Grain, Oatbake, Pop Tarts, Product 19, Raisin Bran, Rice Krispies, Shredded Wheat Squares, Special K			
EXTRAS	Animal testing: non-medical purposes, significant alternative efforts; Corporate Conscience Awards - Employer Responsiveness, Disclosure; Direct investment in South Africa			

BREAKFAST FOOD

COMPANIES	ENVIRONMENT	MINORITIES	WOMEN	DISCLOSURE
PET INC.	I	I	C	F

PRODUCTS OR SUBSIDIARIES: Downyflake

COMPANIES	ENVIRONMENT	MINORITIES	WOMEN	DISCLOSURE
PHILIP MORRIS	F	A	A	F

PRODUCTS OR SUBSIDIARIES: Frosted Rice Krinkles, Fruit & Fibre, Grape-Nuts, Honey Bunches of Oats, Honey Nut Crunch, Honeycomb, Light n' Lively, Post Grape Nuts, Post Raisin Bran

EXTRAS: Animal testing: non-medical purposes; Cigarettes; Indirect ties to South Africa; Workplace Principles

COMPANIES	ENVIRONMENT	MINORITIES	WOMEN	DISCLOSURE
QUAKER OATS	C	A	A	A

PRODUCTS OR SUBSIDIARIES: Aunt Jemima pancake mixes and, Cap'n Crunch, Life cereal, Oh's, Quaker 100% Natural cereal, Quaker Oat Squares, Quaker Oatmeal

EXTRAS: Fair Share

COMPANIES	ENVIRONMENT	MINORITIES	WOMEN	DISCLOSURE
RALSTON PURINA	F	A	C	A

PRODUCTS OR SUBSIDIARIES: Chex, Cookie Crisp, Muesli, Teenage Mutant Ninja Turtles

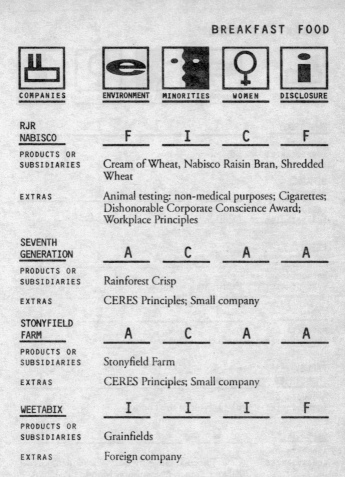

COMPANIES	ENVIRONMENT	MINORITIES	WOMEN	DISCLOSURE
RJR NABISCO	F	I	C	F
PRODUCTS OR SUBSIDIARIES	Cream of Wheat, Nabisco Raisin Bran, Shredded Wheat			
EXTRAS	Animal testing: non-medical purposes; Cigarettes; Dishonorable Corporate Conscience Award; Workplace Principles			
SEVENTH GENERATION	A	C	A	A
PRODUCTS OR SUBSIDIARIES	Rainforest Crisp			
EXTRAS	CERES Principles; Small company			
STONYFIELD FARM	A	C	A	A
PRODUCTS OR SUBSIDIARIES	Stonyfield Farm			
EXTRAS	CERES Principles; Small company			
WEETABIX	I	I	I	F
PRODUCTS OR SUBSIDIARIES	Grainfields			
EXTRAS	Foreign company			

CLOTHING LABELS

BENETTON GROUP	I	I	I	F
PRODUCTS OR SUBSIDIARIES	Benetton clothing			
EXTRAS	Foreign company			

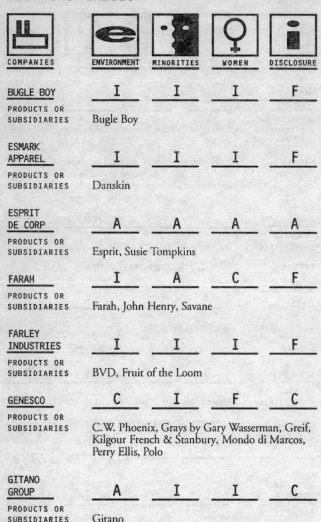

COMPANIES	ENVIRONMENT	MINORITIES	WOMEN	DISCLOSURE
BUGLE BOY	I	I	I	F
PRODUCTS OR SUBSIDIARIES	Bugle Boy			
ESMARK APPAREL	I	I	I	F
PRODUCTS OR SUBSIDIARIES	Danskin			
ESPRIT DE CORP	A	A	A	A
PRODUCTS OR SUBSIDIARIES	Esprit, Susie Tompkins			
FARAH	I	A	C	F
PRODUCTS OR SUBSIDIARIES	Farah, John Henry, Savane			
FARLEY INDUSTRIES	I	I	I	F
PRODUCTS OR SUBSIDIARIES	BVD, Fruit of the Loom			
GENESCO	C	I	F	C
PRODUCTS OR SUBSIDIARIES	C.W. Phoenix, Grays by Gary Wasserman, Greif, Kilgour French & Stanbury, Mondo di Marcos, Perry Ellis, Polo			
GITANO GROUP	A	I	I	C
PRODUCTS OR SUBSIDIARIES	Gitano			

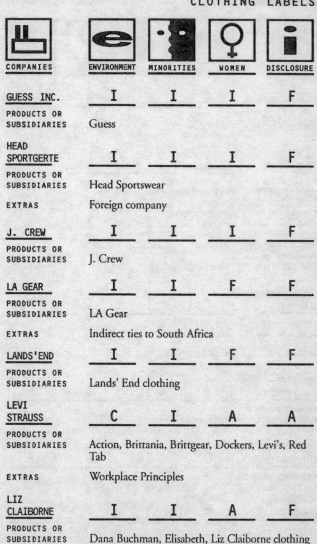

COMPANIES	ENVIRONMENT	MINORITIES	WOMEN	DISCLOSURE
GUESS INC.	I	I	I	F
PRODUCTS OR SUBSIDIARIES	Guess			
HEAD SPORTGERTE	I	I	I	F
PRODUCTS OR SUBSIDIARIES	Head Sportswear			
EXTRAS	Foreign company			
J. CREW	I	I	I	F
PRODUCTS OR SUBSIDIARIES	J. Crew			
LA GEAR	I	I	F	F
PRODUCTS OR SUBSIDIARIES	LA Gear			
EXTRAS	Indirect ties to South Africa			
LANDS'END	I	I	F	F
PRODUCTS OR SUBSIDIARIES	Lands' End clothing			
LEVI STRAUSS	C	I	A	A
PRODUCTS OR SUBSIDIARIES	Action, Brittania, Brittgear, Dockers, Levi's, Red Tab			
EXTRAS	Workplace Principles			
LIZ CLAIBORNE	I	I	A	F
PRODUCTS OR SUBSIDIARIES	Dana Buchman, Elisabeth, Liz Claiborne clothing			

CLOTHING LABELS

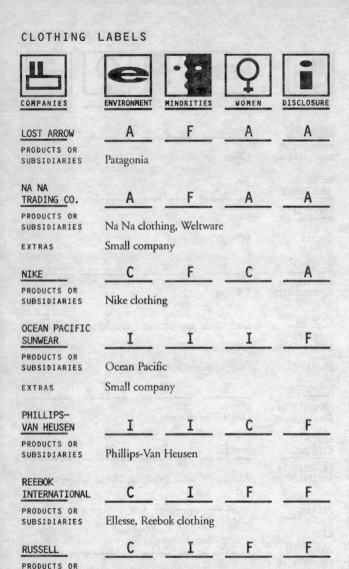

COMPANIES	ENVIRONMENT	MINORITIES	WOMEN	DISCLOSURE	PRODUCTS OR SUBSIDIARIES	EXTRAS
LOST ARROW	A	F	A	A	Patagonia	
NA NA TRADING CO.	A	F	A	A	Na Na clothing, Weltware	Small company
NIKE	C	F	C	A	Nike clothing	
OCEAN PACIFIC SUNWEAR	I	I	I	F	Ocean Pacific	Small company
PHILLIPS-VAN HEUSEN	I	I	C	F	Phillips-Van Heusen	
REEBOK INTERNATIONAL	C	I	F	F	Ellesse, Reebok clothing	
RUSSELL	C	I	F	F	Jerzees, Russell Athletic	

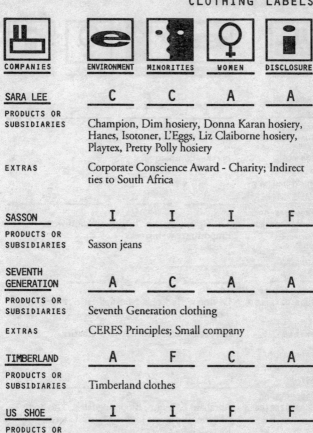

COMPANIES	ENVIRONMENT	MINORITIES	WOMEN	DISCLOSURE
SARA LEE	C	C	A	A
PRODUCTS OR SUBSIDIARIES	Champion, Dim hosiery, Donna Karan hosiery, Hanes, Isotoner, L'Eggs, Liz Claiborne hosiery, Playtex, Pretty Polly hosiery			
EXTRAS	Corporate Conscience Award - Charity; Indirect ties to South Africa			
SASSON	I	I	I	F
PRODUCTS OR SUBSIDIARIES	Sasson jeans			
SEVENTH GENERATION	A	C	A	A
PRODUCTS OR SUBSIDIARIES	Seventh Generation clothing			
EXTRAS	CERES Principles; Small company			
TIMBERLAND	A	F	C	A
PRODUCTS OR SUBSIDIARIES	Timberland clothes			
US SHOE	I	I	F	F
PRODUCTS OR SUBSIDIARIES	Casual Corner, Eastwood Place, L-S-P			
V.F. CORP.	C	I	C	F
PRODUCTS OR SUBSIDIARIES	Barbizon, Basset Walker, Bolero, JanSport, Jantzen, Lee, Lollipop, Marithe Francois Girbaud, O Wear, Rustler, Silhouette, Siltex, Vanity Fair, Variance, Vassarette, Wrangler			

CLOTHING STORES

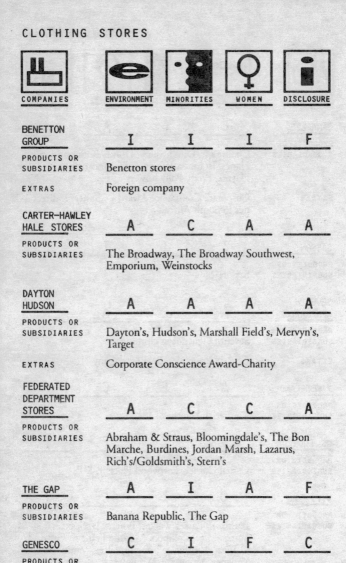

COMPANIES	ENVIRONMENT	MINORITIES	WOMEN	DISCLOSURE
BENETTON GROUP	I	I	I	F
PRODUCTS OR SUBSIDIARIES	Benetton stores			
EXTRAS	Foreign company			
CARTER-HAWLEY HALE STORES	A	C	A	A
PRODUCTS OR SUBSIDIARIES	The Broadway, The Broadway Southwest, Emporium, Weinstocks			
DAYTON HUDSON	A	A	A	A
PRODUCTS OR SUBSIDIARIES	Dayton's, Hudson's, Marshall Field's, Mervyn's, Target			
EXTRAS	Corporate Conscience Award-Charity			
FEDERATED DEPARTMENT STORES	A	C	C	A
PRODUCTS OR SUBSIDIARIES	Abraham & Straus, Bloomingdale's, The Bon Marche, Burdines, Jordan Marsh, Lazarus, Rich's/Goldsmith's, Stern's			
THE GAP	A	I	A	F
PRODUCTS OR SUBSIDIARIES	Banana Republic, The Gap			
GENESCO	C	I	F	C
PRODUCTS OR SUBSIDIARIES	Chaps by Ralph Lauren			

COMPANIES	ENVIRONMENT	MINORITIES	WOMEN	DISCLOSURE
J.C.PENNEY	C	I	C	F
PRODUCTS OR SUBSIDIARIES	J.C. Penney			
K-MART	C	C	A	C
PRODUCTS OR SUBSIDIARIES	K-Mart			
EXTRAS	Fair Share			
THE LIMITED	I	I	A	F
PRODUCTS OR SUBSIDIARIES	Abercrombie & Fitch, Cacique, Express, Henri Bendel, Lane Bryant, Lerner's, Limited, Penhaligon's, Structure, Victoria's Secret			
R.H. MACY	I	I	I	F
PRODUCTS OR SUBSIDIARIES	Bullock's, I. Magnin, Macy's			
EXTRAS	Workplace Principles			
MAY DEPARTMENT STORES	I	C	A	A
PRODUCTS OR SUBSIDIARIES	Filene's, Foley's, Lord & Taylor			
EXTRAS	Workplace Principles			
NORDSTROM	A	A	A	A
PRODUCTS OR SUBSIDIARIES	Nordstrom			

CLOTHING STORES

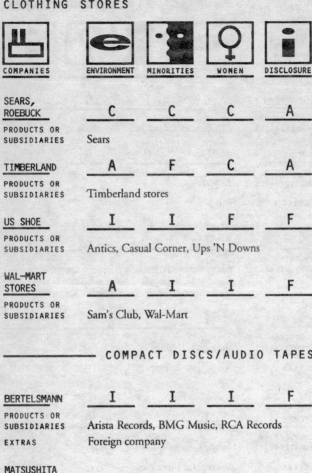

COMPANIES	ENVIRONMENT	MINORITIES	WOMEN	DISCLOSURE
SEARS, ROEBUCK	C	C	C	A
TIMBERLAND	A	F	C	A
US SHOE	I	I	F	F
WAL-MART STORES	A	I	I	F

SEARS, ROEBUCK — PRODUCTS OR SUBSIDIARIES: Sears

TIMBERLAND — PRODUCTS OR SUBSIDIARIES: Timberland stores

US SHOE — PRODUCTS OR SUBSIDIARIES: Antics, Casual Corner, Ups 'N Downs

WAL-MART STORES — PRODUCTS OR SUBSIDIARIES: Sam's Club, Wal-Mart

COMPACT DISCS/AUDIO TAPES

COMPANIES	ENVIRONMENT	MINORITIES	WOMEN	DISCLOSURE
BERTELSMANN	I	I	I	F
MATSUSHITA ELECTRIC INDUSTRIAL	C	I	I	F

BERTELSMANN — PRODUCTS OR SUBSIDIARIES: Arista Records, BMG Music, RCA Records
EXTRAS: Foreign company

MATSUSHITA ELECTRIC INDUSTRIAL — PRODUCTS OR SUBSIDIARIES: DGC Records, Geffen Records, MCA Records
EXTRAS: Fair Share; Foreign company

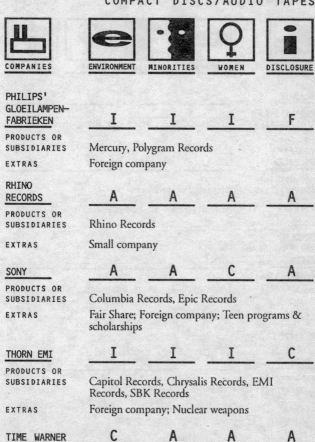

COMPANIES	ENVIRONMENT	MINORITIES	WOMEN	DISCLOSURE
PHILIPS' GLOEILAMPEN-FABRIEKEN	I	I	I	F
RHINO RECORDS	A	A	A	A
SONY	A	A	C	A
THORN EMI	I	I	I	C
TIME WARNER	C	A	A	A

PHILIPS' GLOEILAMPEN-FABRIEKEN

PRODUCTS OR SUBSIDIARIES: Mercury, Polygram Records

EXTRAS: Foreign company

RHINO RECORDS

PRODUCTS OR SUBSIDIARIES: Rhino Records

EXTRAS: Small company

SONY

PRODUCTS OR SUBSIDIARIES: Columbia Records, Epic Records

EXTRAS: Fair Share; Foreign company; Teen programs & scholarships

THORN EMI

PRODUCTS OR SUBSIDIARIES: Capitol Records, Chrysalis Records, EMI Records, SBK Records

EXTRAS: Foreign company; Nuclear weapons

TIME WARNER

PRODUCTS OR SUBSIDIARIES: Atlantic Records, Elektra Records, Warner Bros. Records

EXTRAS: Indirect ties to South Africa; Teen programs & scholarships; Workplace Principles

CONDOMS

COMPANIES	ENVIRONMENT	MINORITIES	WOMEN	DISCLOSURE
ALADAN	I	I	I	F

PRODUCTS OR SUBSIDIARIES: Embrace, Gold Circle Coin, Rainbow, Saxon

COMPANIES	ENVIRONMENT	MINORITIES	WOMEN	DISCLOSURE
CARTER-WALLACE	C	I	F	F

PRODUCTS OR SUBSIDIARIES: Mentor, Poker, Trojan

EXTRAS: Animal testing: medical purposes only

COMPANIES	ENVIRONMENT	MINORITIES	WOMEN	DISCLOSURE
LONDON INTERNATIONAL GROUP	I	I	I	F

PRODUCTS OR SUBSIDIARIES: Durex, Excita, Fourex, Koromex, Protex, Ramses, Sheik

EXTRAS: Foreign company

COMPANIES	ENVIRONMENT	MINORITIES	WOMEN	DISCLOSURE
PACIFIC DUNLOP HOLDING	I	I	I	F

PRODUCTS OR SUBSIDIARIES: Lifestyles

EXTRAS: Foreign company

DENTAL CARE

COMPANIES	ENVIRONMENT	MINORITIES	WOMEN	DISCLOSURE
CADBURY SCHWEPPES	A	I	C	A

PRODUCTS OR SUBSIDIARIES: Murray

EXTRAS: Foreign company

COMPANIES	ENVIRONMENT	MINORITIES	WOMEN	DISCLOSURE
CHURCH & DWIGHT	A	C	C	A

PRODUCTS OR SUBSIDIARIES: Arm & Hammer

EXTRAS: Animal testing: non-medical purposes, significant alternative efforts; Corporate Conscience Award-Environment

COMPANIES	ENVIRONMENT	MINORITIES	WOMEN	DISCLOSURE
COLGATE-PALMOLIVE	A	A	A	A

PRODUCTS OR SUBSIDIARIES: Colgate toothbrushes, Colgate toothpaste, Flourigard, Peak, Ultra Brite

EXTRAS: Animal testing: medical & non-medical purposes, significant alternative efforts; Direct investment in South Africa

COMPANIES	ENVIRONMENT	MINORITIES	WOMEN	DISCLOSURE
GILLETTE	C	C	C	A

PRODUCTS OR SUBSIDIARIES: Oral B

EXTRAS: Animal testing: medical & non-medical purposes, significant alternative efforts

COMPANIES	ENVIRONMENT	MINORITIES	WOMEN	DISCLOSURE
JOHNSON & JOHNSON	C	A	A	A

PRODUCTS OR SUBSIDIARIES: Act, Dental Floss, Prevent, Reach

EXTRAS: Animal testing: medical purposes only, significant alternative efforts; Direct investment in South Africa; Workplace Principles

COMPANIES	ENVIRONMENT	MINORITIES	WOMEN	DISCLOSURE
RJR NABISCO	F	I	C	F

PRODUCTS OR SUBSIDIARIES: Breathsavers

EXTRAS: Animal testing: non-medical purposes; Cigarettes; Dishonorable Corporate Conscience Award; Workplace Principles

COMPANIES	ENVIRONMENT	MINORITIES	WOMEN	DISCLOSURE
PFIZER	F	I	C	F

PRODUCTS OR SUBSIDIARIES: Plax mouthwash

EXTRAS: Animal testing: medical purposes only; Direct investment in South Africa; Workplace Principles

COMPANIES	ENVIRONMENT	MINORITIES	WOMEN	DISCLOSURE
PLAYTEX FP GROUP	I	I	I	F

PRODUCTS OR SUBSIDIARIES: Tek

EXTRAS: Animal testing: non-medical purposes

COMPANIES	ENVIRONMENT	MINORITIES	WOMEN	DISCLOSURE
PROCTER & GAMBLE	C	A	C	A

PRODUCTS OR SUBSIDIARIES: Crest, Denquel, Gleem,Scope

EXTRAS: Animal testing: medical and non-medical purposes, significant alternative efforts; Corporate Conscience Awards - Animal Welfare, Employer Responsiveness; Indirect ties to South Africa; Workplace Principles

DENTAL CARE

COMPANIES	ENVIRONMENT	MINORITIES	WOMEN	DISCLOSURE
RECKITT & COLMAN	I	I	I	F
PRODUCTS OR SUBSIDIARIES	Binaca			
EXTRAS	Animal testing: non-medical purposes; Foreign company			
TOM'S OF MAINE	A	C	A	A
PRODUCTS OR SUBSIDIARIES	Tom's of Maine			
EXTRAS	CERES Principles; Corporate Conscience Award-Charity; Small company			
UNILEVER	C	F	F	A
PRODUCTS OR SUBSIDIARIES	Aim, Close-Up, Signal			
EXTRAS	Animal testing: non-medical purposes, significant alternative efforts; Foreign company			
WARNER-LAMBERT	C	A	C	A
PRODUCTS OR SUBSIDIARIES	Certs, Listermint			
EXTRAS	Animal testing: medical purposes only; Direct investment in South Africa; Workplace Principles			

DEODORANT

COMPANIES	ENVIRONMENT	MINORITIES	WOMEN	DISCLOSURE
ALBERTO-CULVER	C	F	A	A
PRODUCTS OR SUBSIDIARIES	Consort deodorant			
EXTRAS	Animal testing: non-medical purposes			

DEODORANTS

COMPANIES	ENVIRONMENT	MINORITIES	WOMEN	DISCLOSURE
BRISTOL-MYERS SQUIBB	C	A	C	A

PRODUCTS OR SUBSIDIARIES: Ban

EXTRAS: Animal testing: medical & non-medical purposes, significant alternative efforts; Direct investment in South Africa; Infant formula; Workplace Principles

COMPANIES	ENVIRONMENT	MINORITIES	WOMEN	DISCLOSURE
CARTER-WALLACE	C	I	F	F

PRODUCTS OR SUBSIDIARIES: Arrid, Lady's Choice

EXTRAS: Animal testing: medical purposes only

COMPANIES	ENVIRONMENT	MINORITIES	WOMEN	DISCLOSURE
COLGATE-PALMOLIVE	A	A	A	A

PRODUCTS OR SUBSIDIARIES: Irish Spring deodorant, Mennen, Teen Spirit

EXTRAS: Animal testing: medical & non-medical purposes, significant alternative efforts; Direct investment in South Africa

COMPANIES	ENVIRONMENT	MINORITIES	WOMEN	DISCLOSURE
EASTMAN KODAK	F	A	A	A

PRODUCTS OR SUBSIDIARIES: Tussy

EXTRAS: Animal testing: medical and non-medical purposes, significant alternative efforts; Corporate Conscience Award - EEO

COMPANIES	ENVIRONMENT	MINORITIES	WOMEN	DISCLOSURE
GILLETTE	C	C	C	A

PRODUCTS OR SUBSIDIARIES: Dry Idea, Right Guard, Soft and Dri

EXTRAS: Animal testing: medical & non-medical purposes, significant alternative efforts

COMPANIES	ENVIRONMENT	MINORITIES	WOMEN	DISCLOSURE
HELENE CURTIS	A	I	C	C

PRODUCTS OR SUBSIDIARIES: Degree

EXTRAS: Animal testing: non-medical purposes

COMPANIES	ENVIRONMENT	MINORITIES	WOMEN	DISCLOSURE
PROCTER & GAMBLE	C	A	C	A

PRODUCTS OR SUBSIDIARIES: Old Spice, Secret, Sure

EXTRAS: Animal testing: medical and non-medical purposes, significant alternative efforts; Corporate Conscience Awards - Animal Welfare, Employer Responsiveness; Indirect ties to South Africa; Workplace Principles

COMPANIES	ENVIRONMENT	MINORITIES	WOMEN	DISCLOSURE
TOM'S OF MAINE	A	C	A	A

PRODUCTS OR SUBSIDIARIES: Tom's of Maine

EXTRAS: CERES Principles; Corporate Conscience Award-Charity; Small company

COMPANIES	ENVIRONMENT	MINORITIES	WOMEN	DISCLOSURE
UNILEVER	C	F	F	A

PRODUCTS OR SUBSIDIARIES: Faberge

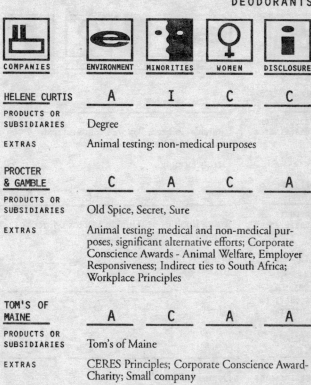

EXTRAS: Animal testing: non-medical purposes, significant alternative efforts; Foreign company

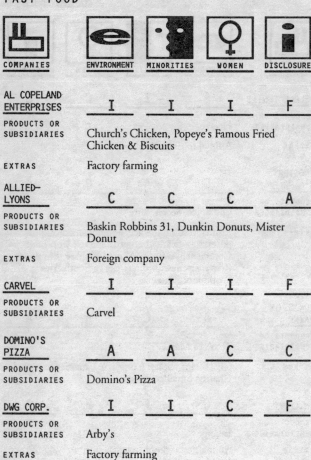

COMPANIES	ENVIRONMENT	MINORITIES	WOMEN	DISCLOSURE
AL COPELAND ENTERPRISES	I	I	I	F
PRODUCTS OR SUBSIDIARIES	Church's Chicken, Popeye's Famous Fried Chicken & Biscuits			
EXTRAS	Factory farming			
ALLIED-LYONS	C	C	C	A
PRODUCTS OR SUBSIDIARIES	Baskin Robbins 31, Dunkin Donuts, Mister Donut			
EXTRAS	Foreign company			
CARVEL	I	I	I	F
PRODUCTS OR SUBSIDIARIES	Carvel			
DOMINO'S PIZZA	A	A	C	C
PRODUCTS OR SUBSIDIARIES	Domino's Pizza			
DWG CORP.	I	I	C	F
PRODUCTS OR SUBSIDIARIES	Arby's			
EXTRAS	Factory farming			
GRAND METROPOLITAN	C	A	C	A
PRODUCTS OR SUBSIDIARIES	Burger King			
EXTRAS	Factory farming; Foreign company; Teen programs & scholarships			

COMPANIES	ENVIRONMENT	MINORITIES	WOMEN	DISCLOSURE
IMASCO	I	F	C	F
PRODUCTS OR SUBSIDIARIES	Hardee's, Roy Rogers			
EXTRAS	Factory farming; Fair Share; Foreign company			
INTERNATIONAL DAIRY QUEEN	C	F	C	A
PRODUCTS OR SUBSIDIARIES	Dairy Queen, Golden Skillet, Karmelkorn, Orange Julius			
MCDONALD'S	C	A	C	C
PRODUCTS OR SUBSIDIARIES	McDonald's			
EXTRAS	Factory farming; Fair Share; Teen programs & scholarships			
PEPSICO	C	A	A	A
PRODUCTS OR SUBSIDIARIES	Kentucky Fried Chicken, Pizza Hut, Taco Bell			
EXTRAS	Animal testing: non-medical purposes; Factory farming; Indirect ties to South Africa; Teen programs & scholarships			
WENDY'S INTERNATIONAL	A	I	A	C
PRODUCTS OR SUBSIDIARIES	Wendy's			
EXTRAS	Factory farming; Fair Share			

COMPANIES	ENVIRONMENT	MINORITIES	WOMEN	DISCLOSURE
AMOCO	F	C	C	A

PRODUCTS OR SUBSIDIARIES: Amoco

EXTRAS: Animal testing: medical & non-medical purposes; Corporate Conscience Award - Community

COMPANIES	ENVIRONMENT	MINORITIES	WOMEN	DISCLOSURE
ATLANTIC RICHFIELD	F	C	A	C

PRODUCTS OR SUBSIDIARIES: ARCO

EXTRAS: Animal testing: non-medical purposes

COMPANIES	ENVIRONMENT	MINORITIES	WOMEN	DISCLOSURE
BRITISH PETROLEUM	F	F	C	A

PRODUCTS OR SUBSIDIARIES: BP America

EXTRAS: Animal testing: non-medical purposes, significant alternative efforts; Direct investment in South Africa; Foreign company; Workplace Principles

COMPANIES	ENVIRONMENT	MINORITIES	WOMEN	DISCLOSURE
CHEVRON	F	A	F	A

PRODUCTS OR SUBSIDIARIES: Chevron

EXTRAS: Animal testing: non-medical purposes, significant alternative efforts; Direct investment in South Africa; Pesticides; Workplace Principles

COMPANIES	ENVIRONMENT	MINORITIES	WOMEN	DISCLOSURE
EXXON CORP.	F	C	C	A

PRODUCTS OR SUBSIDIARIES: Exxon

EXTRAS: Animal testing: non-medical purposes, significant alternative efforts; Dishonorable Corporate Conscience Award

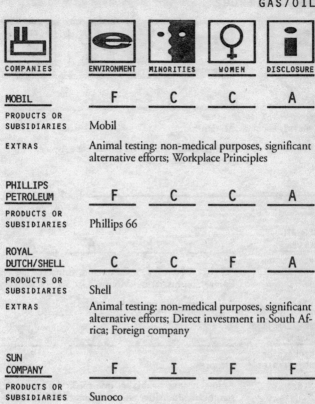

COMPANIES	ENVIRONMENT	MINORITIES	WOMEN	DISCLOSURE
MOBIL	F	C	C	A
PRODUCTS OR SUBSIDIARIES	Mobil			
EXTRAS	Animal testing: non-medical purposes, significant alternative efforts; Workplace Principles			
PHILLIPS PETROLEUM	F	C	C	A
PRODUCTS OR SUBSIDIARIES	Phillips 66			
ROYAL DUTCH/SHELL	C	C	F	A
PRODUCTS OR SUBSIDIARIES	Shell			
EXTRAS	Animal testing: non-medical purposes, significant alternative efforts; Direct investment in South Africa; Foreign company			
SUN COMPANY	F	I	F	F
PRODUCTS OR SUBSIDIARIES	Sunoco			
TEXACO	F	F	F	A
PRODUCTS OR SUBSIDIARIES	Texaco			
EXTRAS	Animal testing: non-medical purposes; Direct investment in South Africa			

GAS/OIL

COMPANIES	ENVIRONMENT	MINORITIES	WOMEN	DISCLOSURE
USX CORP.	F	F	F	F

PRODUCTS OR SUBSIDIARIES: Marathon

EXTRAS: Dishonorable Corporate Conscience Award; Indirect ties to South Africa

HAIR CARE

COMPANIES	ENVIRONMENT	MINORITIES	WOMEN	DISCLOSURE
ALBERTO-CULVER	C	F	A	A

PRODUCTS OR SUBSIDIARIES: Alberto, Alberto VO5, Command, Consort Hair Spray, Consort Styling Mousse, Get Set, TCB

EXTRAS: Animal testing: non-medical purposes

COMPANIES	ENVIRONMENT	MINORITIES	WOMEN	DISCLOSURE
AMERICAN HOME PRODUCTS	F	F	C	A

PRODUCTS OR SUBSIDIARIES: Denorex

EXTRAS: Animal testing: medical & non-medical purposes, significant alternative efforts; Infant formula; Indirect ties to South Africa

COMPANIES	ENVIRONMENT	MINORITIES	WOMEN	DISCLOSURE
AVEDA	A	A	A	A

PRODUCTS OR SUBSIDIARIES: Aveda hair and skin care

EXTRAS: CERES Principles

COMPANIES	ENVIRONMENT	MINORITIES	WOMEN	DISCLOSURE
THE BODY SHOP	A	C	A	A

PRODUCTS OR SUBSIDIARIES: Body Shop shampoo

EXTRAS: Foreign company

COMPANIES	ENVIRONMENT	MINORITIES	WOMEN	DISCLOSURE
BRISTOL-MYERS SQUIBB	C	A	C	A

PRODUCTS OR SUBSIDIARIES: Clairol, Final Net, Herbal Essence, Infusium 23, Instant Beauty

EXTRAS: Animal testing: medical & non-medical purposes, significant alternative efforts; Direct investment in South Africa; Infant formula; Workplace Principles

COMPANIES	ENVIRONMENT	MINORITIES	WOMEN	DISCLOSURE
CARTER-WALLACE	C	I	F	F

PRODUCTS OR SUBSIDIARIES: Linco Beer, Rilacrin, Sue Pree

EXTRAS: Animal testing: medical purposes only

COMPANIES	ENVIRONMENT	MINORITIES	WOMEN	DISCLOSURE
COLGATE-PALMOLIVE	A	A	A	A

PRODUCTS OR SUBSIDIARIES: Baby Magic shampoo, Protein 21, Wildroot

EXTRAS: Animal testing: medical & non-medical purposes, significant alternative efforts; Direct investment in South Africa

COMPANIES	ENVIRONMENT	MINORITIES	WOMEN	DISCLOSURE
GILLETTE	C	C	C	A

PRODUCTS OR SUBSIDIARIES: White Rain

EXTRAS: Animal testing: medical & non-medical purposes, significant alternative efforts

COMPANIES	ENVIRONMENT	MINORITIES	WOMEN	DISCLOSURE
HELENE CURTIS	A	I	C	C

PRODUCTS OR SUBSIDIARIES: Finesse, Salon Selectives, Suave, Vibrance

EXTRAS: Animal testing: non-medical purposes

HAIR CARE

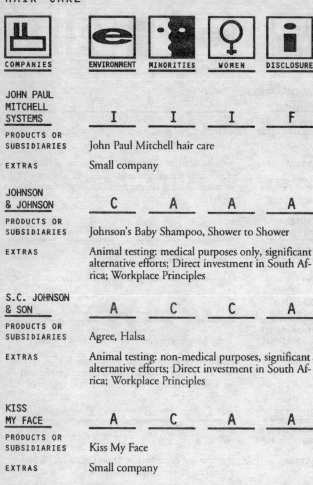

COMPANIES	ENVIRONMENT	MINORITIES	WOMEN	DISCLOSURE
JOHN PAUL MITCHELL SYSTEMS	I	I	I	F

PRODUCTS OR SUBSIDIARIES: John Paul Mitchell hair care

EXTRAS: Small company

COMPANIES	ENVIRONMENT	MINORITIES	WOMEN	DISCLOSURE
JOHNSON & JOHNSON	C	A	A	A

PRODUCTS OR SUBSIDIARIES: Johnson's Baby Shampoo, Shower to Shower

EXTRAS: Animal testing: medical purposes only, significant alternative efforts; Direct investment in South Africa; Workplace Principles

COMPANIES	ENVIRONMENT	MINORITIES	WOMEN	DISCLOSURE
S.C. JOHNSON & SON	A	C	C	A

PRODUCTS OR SUBSIDIARIES: Agree, Halsa

EXTRAS: Animal testing: non-medical purposes, significant alternative efforts; Direct investment in South Africa; Workplace Principles

COMPANIES	ENVIRONMENT	MINORITIES	WOMEN	DISCLOSURE
KISS MY FACE	A	C	A	A

PRODUCTS OR SUBSIDIARIES: Kiss My Face

EXTRAS: Small company

COMPANIES	ENVIRONMENT	MINORITIES	WOMEN	DISCLOSURE
L'OREAL	C	C	A	A

PRODUCTS OR SUBSIDIARIES: L'Oreal shampoo

EXTRAS: Animal testing: non-medical purposes, significant alternative efforts; Foreign company

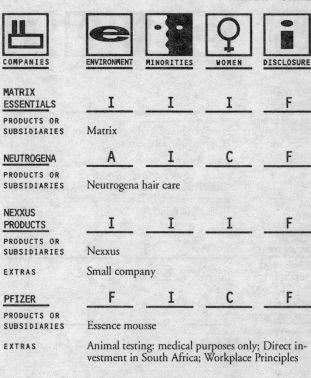

COMPANIES	ENVIRONMENT	MINORITIES	WOMEN	DISCLOSURE
MATRIX ESSENTIALS	I	I	I	F
PRODUCTS OR SUBSIDIARIES	Matrix			
NEUTROGENA	A	I	C	F
PRODUCTS OR SUBSIDIARIES	Neutrogena hair care			
NEXXUS PRODUCTS	I	I	I	F
PRODUCTS OR SUBSIDIARIES	Nexxus			
EXTRAS	Small company			
PFIZER	F	I	C	F
PRODUCTS OR SUBSIDIARIES	Essence mousse			
EXTRAS	Animal testing: medical purposes only; Direct investment in South Africa; Workplace Principles			
PLAYTEX FP GROUP	I	I	I	F
PRODUCTS OR SUBSIDIARIES	Jhirmack			
EXTRAS	Animal testing: non-medical purposes			

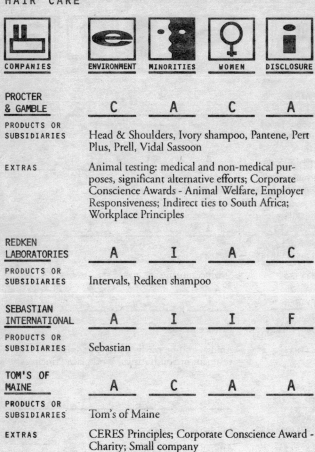

COMPANIES	ENVIRONMENT	MINORITIES	WOMEN	DISCLOSURE
PROCTER & GAMBLE	C	A	C	A
REDKEN LABORATORIES	A	I	A	C
SEBASTIAN INTERNATIONAL	A	I	I	F
TOM'S OF MAINE	A	C	A	A
UNILEVER	C	F	F	A

PROCTER & GAMBLE

PRODUCTS OR SUBSIDIARIES: Head & Shoulders, Ivory shampoo, Pantene, Pert Plus, Prell, Vidal Sassoon

EXTRAS: Animal testing: medical and non-medical purposes, significant alternative efforts; Corporate Conscience Awards - Animal Welfare, Employer Responsiveness; Indirect ties to South Africa; Workplace Principles

REDKEN LABORATORIES

PRODUCTS OR SUBSIDIARIES: Intervals, Redken shampoo

SEBASTIAN INTERNATIONAL

PRODUCTS OR SUBSIDIARIES: Sebastian

TOM'S OF MAINE

PRODUCTS OR SUBSIDIARIES: Tom's of Maine

EXTRAS: CERES Principles; Corporate Conscience Award - Charity; Small company

UNILEVER

PRODUCTS OR SUBSIDIARIES: Aqua Net, Timotei

EXTRAS: Animal testing: non-medical purposes, significant alternative efforts; Foreign company

COMPANIES	ENVIRONMENT	MINORITIES	WOMEN	DISCLOSURE
AMERICAN HOME PRODUCTS	F	F	C	A
AROMA VERA	A	A	A	A
AVON	C	A	A	A
BODY LOVE NATURAL COSMETICS	A	A	A	A

AMERICAN HOME PRODUCTS

PRODUCTS OR SUBSIDIARIES: Compound W

EXTRAS: Animal testing: medical & non-medical purposes, significant alternative efforts; Infant formula; Indirect ties to South Africa

AROMA VERA

PRODUCTS OR SUBSIDIARIES: Aroma Vera

EXTRAS: Small company

AVON

PRODUCTS OR SUBSIDIARIES: Avon, Bioadvance, Charisma, Clear Skin II, Cool Confidence, Daily Revival, Fancy Feet, Feelin' Fresh, Giorgio, Silver Lights, Simply Brilliant, Skin-So-Soft, Soft Essentials, Sun Seekers

EXTRAS: Corporate Conscience Award - Equal Employment Opportunity

BODY LOVE NATURAL COSMETICS

PRODUCTS OR SUBSIDIARIES: Amazing Grains, Aroma Lotion, Aroma Oil, Herbal Facial Steams, Juniper Tonic Massage Oil, Love Mitts

EXTRAS: Small company

MAKEUP/SKIN CARE

COMPANIES	ENVIRONMENT	MINORITIES	WOMEN	DISCLOSURE
THE BODY SHOP	A	C	A	A

PRODUCTS OR SUBSIDIARIES: Body Shop makeup and skin care

EXTRAS: Foreign company

COMPANIES	ENVIRONMENT	MINORITIES	WOMEN	DISCLOSURE
BRISTOL-MYERS SQUIBB	C	A	C	A

PRODUCTS OR SUBSIDIARIES: Ammens, Fostex, Keri Lotion, PreSun, Sea Breeze

EXTRAS: Animal testing: medical & non-medical purposes, significant alternative efforts; Direct investment in South Africa; Infant formula; Workplace Principles

COMPANIES	ENVIRONMENT	MINORITIES	WOMEN	DISCLOSURE
CARTER-WALLACE	C	I	F	F

PRODUCTS OR SUBSIDIARIES: Nair, Sea & Ski

EXTRAS: Animal testing: medical purposes only

COMPANIES	ENVIRONMENT	MINORITIES	WOMEN	DISCLOSURE
COLGATE-PALMOLIVE	A	A	A	A

PRODUCTS OR SUBSIDIARIES: Afta Skin Conditioner, Baby Magic skin care, Balm Barr, Brushless Shave, Colgate shaving cream, Hawk After Shave, Irish Spring soap, Lather Shave, Medicated Face Conditioner, Millionaire After Shave, Palmolive, Skin Bracer, Sof' Stroke, Softsoap

EXTRAS: Animal testing: medical & non-medical purposes, significant alternative efforts; Direct investment in South Africa

COMPANIES	ENVIRONMENT	MINORITIES	WOMEN	DISCLOSURE
EASTMAN KODAK	F	A	A	A

PRODUCTS OR SUBSIDIARIES: PHiso-Derm, Stri-Dex

EXTRAS: Animal testing: medical and non-medical purposes, significant alternative efforts; Corporate Conscience Award -EEO

COMPANIES	ENVIRONMENT	MINORITIES	WOMEN	DISCLOSURE
ECCO BELLA	A	C	A	A

PRODUCTS OR SUBSIDIARIES: Ecco Bella

EXTRAS: Small company

COMPANIES	ENVIRONMENT	MINORITIES	WOMEN	DISCLOSURE
ESTEE LAUDER	A	I	A	C

PRODUCTS OR SUBSIDIARIES: Aramis, Clinique, Estee Lauder, Origins, Prescriptives

EXTRAS: Direct investment in South Africa

COMPANIES	ENVIRONMENT	MINORITIES	WOMEN	DISCLOSURE
GILLETTE	C	C	C	A

PRODUCTS OR SUBSIDIARIES: Jafra

EXTRAS: Animal testing: medical & non-medical purposes, significant alternative efforts

COMPANIES	ENVIRONMENT	MINORITIES	WOMEN	DISCLOSURE
HELENE CURTIS	A	I	C	C

PRODUCTS OR SUBSIDIARIES: Suave

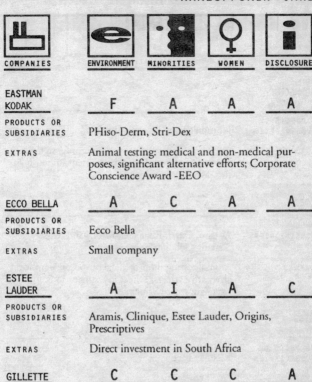

EXTRAS: Animal testing: non-medical purposes

COMPANIES	ENVIRONMENT	MINORITIES	WOMEN	DISCLOSURE
JOHNSON & JOHNSON	C	A	A	A
PRODUCTS OR SUBSIDIARIES	Johnson's Baby Powder, Sundown			
EXTRAS	Animal testing: medical purposes only, significant alternative efforts; Direct investment in South Africa; Workplace Principles			
S.C. JOHNSON & SON	A	C	C	A
PRODUCTS OR SUBSIDIARIES	Aveeno, Curel, Edge Gel, Rhuli, Soft Sense Shaving Gel, Soft Sense lotion			
EXTRAS	Animal testing: non-medical purposes, significant alternative efforts; Direct investment in South Africa; Workplace Principles			
KISS MY FACE	A	C	A	A
PRODUCTS OR SUBSIDIARIES	Kiss My Face			
EXTRAS	Small company			
L'OREAL	C	C	A	A
PRODUCTS OR SUBSIDIARIES	Biotherm, L'Oreal makeup, L'Oreal skin care, Lancome			
EXTRAS	Animal testing: non-medical purposes, significant alternative efforts; Foreign company			
MEM CO.	I	I	A	C
PRODUCTS OR SUBSIDIARIES	Love's			

COMPANIES	ENVIRONMENT	MINORITIES	WOMEN	DISCLOSURE
MINN. MINING & MFG. (3M)	C	A	A	A

PRODUCTS OR SUBSIDIARIES: Buf Puf

EXTRAS: Animal testing: medical & non-medical purposes; Direct investment in South Africa

COMPANIES	ENVIRONMENT	MINORITIES	WOMEN	DISCLOSURE
NEUTROGENA	A	I	C	F

PRODUCTS OR SUBSIDIARIES: Neutrogena skin care

COMPANIES	ENVIRONMENT	MINORITIES	WOMEN	DISCLOSURE
ORJENE NATURAL COSMETICS	A	A	A	A

PRODUCTS OR SUBSIDIARIES: Avocado Oils, Orjene Natural Cosmetics, Vit-A-Skin Cream

EXTRAS: Small company

COMPANIES	ENVIRONMENT	MINORITIES	WOMEN	DISCLOSURE
PFIZER	F	I	C	F

PRODUCTS OR SUBSIDIARIES: Barbasol

EXTRAS: Animal testing: medical purposes only; Direct investment in South Africa; Workplace Principles

COMPANIES	ENVIRONMENT	MINORITIES	WOMEN	DISCLOSURE
PROCTER & GAMBLE	C	A	C	A

PRODUCTS OR SUBSIDIARIES: Bain de Soleil, Camay, Clarion, Clearasil, Coast, Cover Girl, Ivory soap, Kirk's, Max Factor, Noxzema, Oil of Olay, Rain Tree, Safeguard, Wondra, Zest

EXTRAS: Animal testing: medical and non-medical purposes, significant alternative efforts; Corporate Conscience Awards - Animal Welfare, Employer Responsiveness; Indirect ties to South Africa; Workplace Principles

COMPANIES	ENVIRONMENT	MINORITIES	WOMEN	DISCLOSURE
RACHEL PERRY	A	A	A	A

PRODUCTS OR SUBSIDIARIES: Rachel Perry

EXTRAS: Small company

COMPANIES	ENVIRONMENT	MINORITIES	WOMEN	DISCLOSURE
RECKITT & COLMAN	I	I	I	F

PRODUCTS OR SUBSIDIARIES: Neet

EXTRAS: Animal testing: non-medical purposes; Foreign company

COMPANIES	ENVIRONMENT	MINORITIES	WOMEN	DISCLOSURE
REDKEN LABORATORIES	A	I	A	C

PRODUCTS OR SUBSIDIARIES: Redken skin care

COMPANIES	ENVIRONMENT	MINORITIES	WOMEN	DISCLOSURE
REVLON	C	I	I	F

PRODUCTS OR SUBSIDIARIES: Alexandra de Markoff, Almay, Bill Blass, Charles of the Ritz, Halston, New Essentials, Revlon, Roux, Ultima II

COMPANIES	ENVIRONMENT	MINORITIES	WOMEN	DISCLOSURE
SCHERING-PLOUGH	C	A	C	A

PRODUCTS OR SUBSIDIARIES: A & D Ointment, Complex 15, Coppertone, Shade, Solarcaine, Tropical Blend, Zinka,

EXTRAS: Animal testing: medical & non-medical purposes, significant alternative efforts; Direct investment in South Africa; Workplace Principles

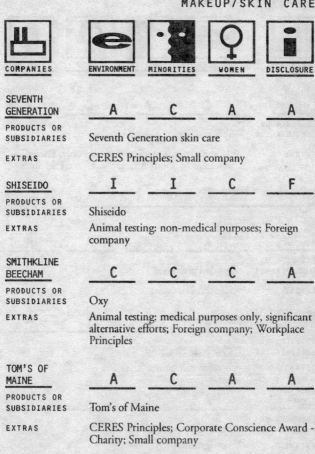

COMPANIES	ENVIRONMENT	MINORITIES	WOMEN	DISCLOSURE
SEVENTH GENERATION	A	C	A	A
PRODUCTS OR SUBSIDIARIES	Seventh Generation skin care			
EXTRAS	CERES Principles; Small company			
SHISEIDO	I	I	C	F
PRODUCTS OR SUBSIDIARIES	Shiseido			
EXTRAS	Animal testing: non-medical purposes; Foreign company			
SMITHKLINE BEECHAM	C	C	C	A
PRODUCTS OR SUBSIDIARIES	Oxy			
EXTRAS	Animal testing: medical purposes only, significant alternative efforts; Foreign company; Workplace Principles			
TOM'S OF MAINE	A	C	A	A
PRODUCTS OR SUBSIDIARIES	Tom's of Maine			
EXTRAS	CERES Principles; Corporate Conscience Award - Charity; Small company			
UNILEVER	C	F	F	A
PRODUCTS OR SUBSIDIARIES	Calvin Klein, Caress, Cutex, Dove, Elizabeth Arden makeup, Lux, Pond's, Shield, Vaseline			
EXTRAS	Animal testing: non-medical purposes, significant alternative efforts; Foreign company			

COMPANIES	ENVIRONMENT	MINORITIES	WOMEN	DISCLOSURE
WARNER-LAMBERT	C	A	C	A

PRODUCTS OR SUBSIDIARIES: Personal Touch, Schick

EXTRAS: Animal testing: medical purposes only; Direct investment in South Africa; Workplace Principles

PERFUME

COMPANIES	ENVIRONMENT	MINORITIES	WOMEN	DISCLOSURE
AVEDA	A	A	A	A

PRODUCTS OR SUBSIDIARIES: Aveda Purefumes

EXTRAS: CERES Principles

COMPANIES	ENVIRONMENT	MINORITIES	WOMEN	DISCLOSURE
BENETTON GROUP	I	I	I	F

PRODUCTS OR SUBSIDIARIES: Colors de Benetton

EXTRAS: Foreign company

COMPANIES	ENVIRONMENT	MINORITIES	WOMEN	DISCLOSURE
THE BODY SHOP	A	C	A	A

PRODUCTS OR SUBSIDIARIES: Body Shop perfume

EXTRAS: Foreign company

COMPANIES	ENVIRONMENT	MINORITIES	WOMEN	DISCLOSURE
ESTEE LAUDER	A	I	A	C

PRODUCTS OR SUBSIDIARIES: White Linen

EXTRAS: Direct investment in South Africa

COMPANIES	ENVIRONMENT	MINORITIES	WOMEN	DISCLOSURE
LIZ CLAIBORNE	I	I	A	F

PRODUCTS OR SUBSIDIARIES: Liz Claiborne perfume, Realities

COMPANIES	ENVIRONMENT	MINORITIES	WOMEN	DISCLOSURE
L'OREAL	C	C	A	A

PRODUCTS OR SUBSIDIARIES: Anais Anais, Cacharel, Giorgio Armani, Gloria Vanderbilt, Guy Laroche, Paloma Picasso, Ralph Lauren perfume

EXTRAS: Animal testing: non-medical purposes, significant alternative efforts; Foreign company

COMPANIES	ENVIRONMENT	MINORITIES	WOMEN	DISCLOSURE
MEM CO.	I	I	A	C

PRODUCTS OR SUBSIDIARIES: English Leather, Fathom, Heaven Sent

COMPANIES	ENVIRONMENT	MINORITIES	WOMEN	DISCLOSURE
PFIZER	F	I	C	F

PRODUCTS OR SUBSIDIARIES: Exclamation, Iron cologne, L'Effleur, Lady Stetson, Musk for Men, Preferred Stock, Sophia perfume, Stetson

EXTRAS: Animal testing: medical purposes only; Direct investment in South Africa; Workplace Principles

COMPANIES	ENVIRONMENT	MINORITIES	WOMEN	DISCLOSURE
PROCTER & GAMBLE	C	A	C	A

PRODUCTS OR SUBSIDIARIES: California, Hugo Boss, Laura Biagiotti-Roma, Navy by Cover Girl, Old Spice, Toujours Moi, le Jardin

EXTRAS: Animal testing: medical and non-medical purposes, significant alternative efforts; Corporate Conscience Awards - Animal Welfare, Employer Responsiveness; Indirect ties to South Africa; Workplace Principles

PERFUME

COMPANIES	ENVIRONMENT	MINORITIES	WOMEN	DISCLOSURE
UNILEVER	C	F	F	A

PRODUCTS OR SUBSIDIARIES: Brut 33, Elizabeth Arden perfume, Eternity, Obsession

EXTRAS: Animal testing: non-medical purposes, significant alternative efforts; Foreign company

SCHOOL SUPPLIES

COMPANIES	ENVIRONMENT	MINORITIES	WOMEN	DISCLOSURE
A.T.CROSS	I	I	F	F

PRODUCTS OR SUBSIDIARIES: Cross pens & pencils

COMPANIES	ENVIRONMENT	MINORITIES	WOMEN	DISCLOSURE
AVERY DENNISON	I	I	C	F

PRODUCTS OR SUBSIDIARIES: Aigner, Avery, Carter's, Dennison, Glue-Stic, K & M Notebooks

COMPANIES	ENVIRONMENT	MINORITIES	WOMEN	DISCLOSURE
SOCIETE BIC	I	I	I	F

PRODUCTS OR SUBSIDIARIES: Bic

EXTRAS: Foreign company

COMPANIES	ENVIRONMENT	MINORITIES	WOMEN	DISCLOSURE
BORDEN	F	A	C	A

PRODUCTS OR SUBSIDIARIES: Elmer's, Krazy Glue

EXTRAS: Direct investment in South Africa

COMPANIES	ENVIRONMENT	MINORITIES	WOMEN	DISCLOSURE
FABER/CASTELL	I	I	I	F

PRODUCTS OR SUBSIDIARIES: Eberhard Faber

COMPANIES	ENVIRONMENT	MINORITIES	WOMEN	DISCLOSURE
GILLETTE	C	C	C	A

PRODUCTS OR SUBSIDIARIES: Liquid Paper, Paper Mate, Waterman

EXTRAS: Animal testing: medical & non-medical purposes, significant alternative efforts

COMPANIES	ENVIRONMENT	MINORITIES	WOMEN	DISCLOSURE
HALLMARK CARDS	C	C	A	C

PRODUCTS OR SUBSIDIARIES: Hallmark

EXTRAS: Corporate Conscience Awards - Equal Opportunity

COMPANIES	ENVIRONMENT	MINORITIES	WOMEN	DISCLOSURE
KIMBERLY-CLARK	F	A	A	F

PRODUCTS OR SUBSIDIARIES: Chieftain, Classic, Kimberly, Scribe

EXTRAS: Animal testing: non-medical purposes

COMPANIES	ENVIRONMENT	MINORITIES	WOMEN	DISCLOSURE
MEAD	F	C	C	C

PRODUCTS OR SUBSIDIARIES: Mead

EXTRAS: Workplace Principles

COMPANIES	ENVIRONMENT	MINORITIES	WOMEN	DISCLOSURE
MINN. MINING & MFG. (3M)	C	A	A	A

PRODUCTS OR SUBSIDIARIES: Post-It, Scotch

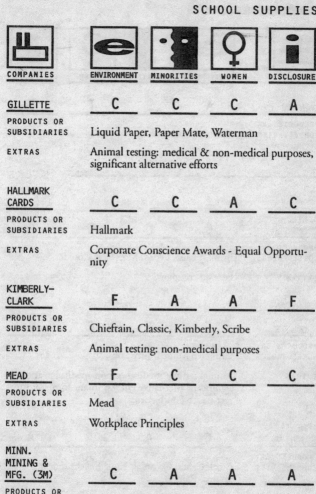

EXTRAS: Animal testing: medical & non-medical purposes; Direct investment in South Africa

SCHOOL SUPPLIES

COMPANIES	ENVIRONMENT	MINORITIES	WOMEN	DISCLOSURE
SANFORD	A	I	I	F

PRODUCTS OR SUBSIDIARIES — Accent, Sanford

SNACKS

COMPANIES	ENVIRONMENT	MINORITIES	WOMEN	DISCLOSURE
ALLIED-LYONS	C	C	C	A

PRODUCTS OR SUBSIDIARIES — Brink, Haust, Lyons, Maryland Cookies

EXTRAS — Foreign company

COMPANIES	ENVIRONMENT	MINORITIES	WOMEN	DISCLOSURE
AMERICAN HOME PRODUCTS	F	F	C	A

PRODUCTS OR SUBSIDIARIES — Crunch'n'Munch, Jiffy Pop

EXTRAS — Animal testing: medical & non-medical purposes, significant alternative efforts; Infant formula; Indirect ties to South Africa

COMPANIES	ENVIRONMENT	MINORITIES	WOMEN	DISCLOSURE
ANHEUSER-BUSCH	C	A	A	A

PRODUCTS OR SUBSIDIARIES — Break Cakes, Colonial, Eagle Snacks, Earth Grains, Rainbo

COMPANIES	ENVIRONMENT	MINORITIES	WOMEN	DISCLOSURE
BEN & JERRY'S	A	C	A	A

PRODUCTS OR SUBSIDIARIES — Ben & Jerry's

EXTRAS — CERES Principles; Corporate Conscience Award - Charity; Workplace Principles

COMPANIES	ENVIRONMENT	MINORITIES	WOMEN	DISCLOSURE
BORDEN	F	A	C	A

PRODUCTS OR SUBSIDIARIES: Borden Ice Cream, Bravo, Buckeye, Cain's, Campfire, Cheez Doodles, Chesty, Clover Club, Cottage Fries, Cracker Jacks, Crane's, Dipsy Doodles, Eagle Brand, El Molino, Fisher, Geiser's, Guy's, Jays, KAS, Krunchers!, La Famous, Little Panchos, Moore's, New York Deli, Old Fashioned Recipe, Pepitos, Ranch Fries, Red Seal, Ridgie's, Seyferts, Snacktime, Turtles, Viva frozen yogurt, Wise

EXTRAS: Direct investment in South Africa

COMPANIES	ENVIRONMENT	MINORITIES	WOMEN	DISCLOSURE
CADBURY SCHWEPPES	A	I	C	A

PRODUCTS OR SUBSIDIARIES: Bassett, Beechnut, Cadbury, Eclairs

EXTRAS: Foreign company

COMPANIES	ENVIRONMENT	MINORITIES	WOMEN	DISCLOSURE
CAMPBELL SOUP	C	A	A	A

PRODUCTS OR SUBSIDIARIES: Godiva, Pepperidge Farm

EXTRAS: Animal testing: non-medical purposes, significant alternative efforts

COMPANIES	ENVIRONMENT	MINORITIES	WOMEN	DISCLOSURE
CONAGRA	F	I	C	F

PRODUCTS OR SUBSIDIARIES: Orville Redenbacher's, Swiss Miss Cocoa

EXTRAS: Dishonorable Corporate Conscience Award; Factory farming

SNACKS

COMPANIES	ENVIRONMENT	MINORITIES	WOMEN	DISCLOSURE
DOLE FOOD	C	C	C	A
PRODUCTS OR SUBSIDIARIES	Dole nuts			
DREYER'S GRAND ICE CREAM	I	I	F	F
PRODUCTS OR SUBSIDIARIES	Dreyer's, Edy's			
R.W. FROOKIES	I	I	I	F
PRODUCTS OR SUBSIDIARIES	R.W. Frookies			
EXTRAS	Small company			
GENERAL MILLS	C	A	A	A
PRODUCTS OR SUBSIDIARIES	Body Buddies, Bugles, Fruit Roll-Ups, Fruit Shapes, Garfield Roll-Ups, Granola Bars, Muffin Mixes, Nature Valley, Pop Secret			
EXTRAS	Corporate Conscience Awards - Charity, Equal Employment Opportunity, Opportunity for the Physically Challenged; Workplace Principles			
GRAND METROPOLITAN	C	A	C	A
PRODUCTS OR SUBSIDIARIES	Haagen Dazs, Jeno's, Pillsbury, Totino's			
EXTRAS	Factory farming; Foreign company; Teen programs & scholarships			

COMPANIES	ENVIRONMENT	MINORITIES	WOMEN	DISCLOSURE
HEALTH VALLEY	A	C	C	A

PRODUCTS OR SUBSIDIARIES — Amaranth Cookies, Apple Bakes, Corn Chips Crisp 'N Natural, Date Bakes, Fancy Fruit Chunks, Fat Free Granola Bars, Fat Free Muffins, Fat Free Organic Whole Wheat, Honey Graham Crackers, Raisin Bakes, Stoned Wheat Crackers

COMPANIES	ENVIRONMENT	MINORITIES	WOMEN	DISCLOSURE
H.J.HEINZ	A	C	C	A

PRODUCTS OR SUBSIDIARIES — Chico-San, Weight Watchers

EXTRAS — Corporate Conscience Award - Environment

COMPANIES	ENVIRONMENT	MINORITIES	WOMEN	DISCLOSURE
HERSHEY FOODS	C	C	C	A

PRODUCTS OR SUBSIDIARIES — 5th Avenue, Bar None, Hershey's, Hershey's Cocoa, Kit Kat, Krackel, Mr. Goodbar, Peter Paul Almond Joy, Peter Paul Mounds, Reese's, Rolo, Skor, Special Dark, Symphony, Whatchamacallit, Y&S Twizzlers, York Peppermint Patties

EXTRAS — Animal testing: non-medical purposes, significant alternative efforts; Hershey School

COMPANIES	ENVIRONMENT	MINORITIES	WOMEN	DISCLOSURE
KELLOGG	A	A	A	A

PRODUCTS OR SUBSIDIARIES — Easy As Pie, Mrs. Smith's, Pie in Minutes, Raisin Squares

EXTRAS — Animal testing: non-medical purposes, significant alternative efforts; Corporate Conscience Awards - Employer Responsiveness, Disclosure; Direct investment in South Africa

SNACKS

COMPANIES	ENVIRONMENT	MINORITIES	WOMEN	DISCLOSURE
MARS	C	I	A	A

PRODUCTS OR SUBSIDIARIES: 3 Musketeers, Combos, Dove, Kudos, M & M's, Mars, Milky Way, Rondos, Skittles, Snickers, Starburst, Summit, Twix

COMPANIES	ENVIRONMENT	MINORITIES	WOMEN	DISCLOSURE
NESTLE	C	I	C	A

PRODUCTS OR SUBSIDIARIES: After Eight Dinner Mints, Baby Ruth, Bon Bons, Butterfinger, Carnation, Chunky, Goobers, Nestle, Nestle Cocoa, Oh Henry!, Quik, Raisinets, Sno-Caps

EXTRAS: Animal testing: non-medical purposes, significant alternative efforts; Direct investment in South Africa; Foreign company; Infant formula

COMPANIES	ENVIRONMENT	MINORITIES	WOMEN	DISCLOSURE
NEWMAN'S OWN	A	C	A	A

PRODUCTS OR SUBSIDIARIES: Newman's popcorn

EXTRAS: 100% profit to charity; Corporate Conscience Award - Charity; Small company

COMPANIES	ENVIRONMENT	MINORITIES	WOMEN	DISCLOSURE
PEPSICO	C	A	A	A

PRODUCTS OR SUBSIDIARIES: Chee-tos, Delta Gold, Doritos, Fritos, FunYuns, Grandma's, Lay's, Munchos, O'Grady's, Rold Gold, Ruffles, Salsa Rio, Smartfood, Tostitos

EXTRAS: Animal testing: non-medical purposes; Factory farming; Indirect ties to South Africa; Teen programs & scholarships

COMPANIES	ENVIRONMENT	MINORITIES	WOMEN	DISCLOSURE
PHILIP MORRIS	F	A	A	F

PRODUCTS OR SUBSIDIARIES: Breyer's, Frusen Gladje, Toblerone

EXTRAS: Animal testing: non-medical purposes; Cigarettes; Indirect ties to South Africa; Workplace Principles

COMPANIES	ENVIRONMENT	MINORITIES	WOMEN	DISCLOSURE
PET INC.	I	I	C	F

PRODUCTS OR SUBSIDIARIES: Whitman's Chocolates

COMPANIES	ENVIRONMENT	MINORITIES	WOMEN	DISCLOSURE
PROCTER & GAMBLE	C	A	C	A

PRODUCTS OR SUBSIDIARIES: Fisher Nuts, Pringles

EXTRAS: Animal testing: medical and non-medical purposes, significant alternative efforts; Corporate Conscience Awards - Animal Welfare, Employer Responsiveness; Indirect ties to South Africa; Workplace Principles

COMPANIES	ENVIRONMENT	MINORITIES	WOMEN	DISCLOSURE
QUAKER OATS	C	A	A	A

PRODUCTS OR SUBSIDIARIES: Celeste Pizza, Granola Dipps, Rice Cakes, Van Camp's products, Whipps

EXTRAS: Fair Share

COMPANIES	ENVIRONMENT	MINORITIES	WOMEN	DISCLOSURE
RALSTON PURINA	F	A	C	A

PRODUCTS OR SUBSIDIARIES: Hostess, Ry Krisp

COMPANIES	ENVIRONMENT	MINORITIES	WOMEN	DISCLOSURE
RECKITT & COLMAN	I	I	I	F

PRODUCTS OR SUBSIDIARIES: Durkee's

EXTRAS: Animal testing: non-medical purposes; Foreign company

COMPANIES	ENVIRONMENT	MINORITIES	WOMEN	DISCLOSURE
RJR NABISCO	F	I	C	F

PRODUCTS OR SUBSIDIARIES: Almost Home, Barnum's Animals, Better Cheddars, Bubble Yum, Carefree, Chips Ahoy, Fig Newtons, Honey Maid, Lifesavers, Mallomars, Newtons, Oreos, Planters, Premium, Ritz, Triscuit, Wheat Thins

EXTRAS: Animal testing: non-medical purposes; Cigarettes; Dishonorable Corporate Conscience Award; Workplace Principles

COMPANIES	ENVIRONMENT	MINORITIES	WOMEN	DISCLOSURE
SARA LEE	C	C	A	A

PRODUCTS OR SUBSIDIARIES: Sara Lee desserts

EXTRAS: Corporate Conscience Award - Charity; Indirect ties to South Africa

COMPANIES	ENVIRONMENT	MINORITIES	WOMEN	DISCLOSURE
SEVENTH GENERATION	A	C	A	A

PRODUCTS OR SUBSIDIARIES: Rainforest Crunch

EXTRAS: CERES Principles; Small company

COMPANIES	ENVIRONMENT	MINORITIES	WOMEN	DISCLOSURE
SUNSHINE BISCUITS	I	I	I	F

PRODUCTS OR SUBSIDIARIES: Bavarian Fingers, Cheez-It, Chip-A-Roos, Country Styles, Doubles, Hydrox, Vienna Fingers

COMPANIES	ENVIRONMENT	MINORITIES	WOMEN	DISCLOSURE
TOPPS CHEWING GUM	I	I	F	F
PRODUCTS OR SUBSIDIARIES	Bazooka, Hockey, Ring Pop, Sundae Cone Candy, Topps, Zooks			
UNILEVER	C	F	F	A
PRODUCTS OR SUBSIDIARIES	Good Humor, Magnum, Popsicle, Sky			
EXTRAS	Animal testing: non-medical purposes, significant alternative efforts; Foreign company			
UNITED BISCUITS	A	F	F	F
PRODUCTS OR SUBSIDIARIES	Chips Deluxe, Elfkins, Hooplas, Keebler, Keebler Soft Batch, Munch'ems, O'Boisies, Pecan Sandies, Pizzarias, Ripplin's, Town House, Wheatables, Zesta			
EXTRAS	Foreign company			
WARNER-LAMBERT	C	A	C	A
PRODUCTS OR SUBSIDIARIES	Bubblicious, Charleston Chew!, Chewels, Chiclets, Clorets, Dentyne, Freshen-Up, Junior Mints, Pom Poms, Sticklets, Sugar Babies, Sugar Daddy, Trident			
EXTRAS	Animal testing: medical purposes only; Direct investment in South Africa; Workplace Principles			

SNACKS

COMPANIES	ENVIRONMENT	MINORITIES	WOMEN	DISCLOSURE
WM. WRIGLEY JR.	C	I	F	F

PRODUCTS OR SUBSIDIARIES: Big League Chew, Big Red, Bubble Tape, Doublemint, Extra Sugarfree Gum, Freedent, Hubba Bubba, Juicy Fruit, Reed Candy Company, Wrigley's

EXTRAS: Fair Share

SNEAKERS/SHOES

COMPANIES	ENVIRONMENT	MINORITIES	WOMEN	DISCLOSURE
ADIDAS	I	I	I	F

PRODUCTS OR SUBSIDIARIES: Adidas

EXTRAS: Foreign company

COMPANIES	ENVIRONMENT	MINORITIES	WOMEN	DISCLOSURE
BIRKENSTOCK FOOTPRINT SANDALS	A	C	A	A

PRODUCTS OR SUBSIDIARIES: Birkenstock Footprint Sandals

COMPANIES	ENVIRONMENT	MINORITIES	WOMEN	DISCLOSURE
BROWN GROUP	I	I	F	F

PRODUCTS OR SUBSIDIARIES: Air Step, Brown, Buster Brown, Naturalizer, Regal

COMPANIES	ENVIRONMENT	MINORITIES	WOMEN	DISCLOSURE
FISHER CAMUTO RETAIL	I	I	I	F

PRODUCTS OR SUBSIDIARIES: Calico, Enzo Angiotini, Gloria Vanderbilt, Jacques Vincent, Nine West, Westies

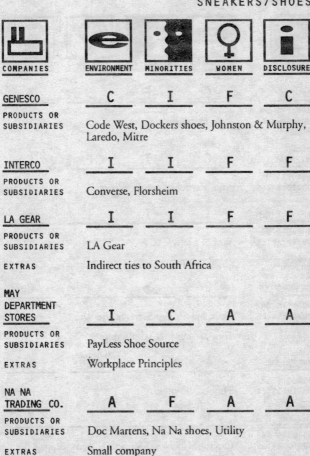

COMPANIES	ENVIRONMENT	MINORITIES	WOMEN	DISCLOSURE
GENESCO	C	I	F	C
PRODUCTS OR SUBSIDIARIES	Code West, Dockers shoes, Johnston & Murphy, Laredo, Mitre			
INTERCO	I	I	F	F
PRODUCTS OR SUBSIDIARIES	Converse, Florsheim			
LA GEAR	I	I	F	F
PRODUCTS OR SUBSIDIARIES	LA Gear			
EXTRAS	Indirect ties to South Africa			
MAY DEPARTMENT STORES	I	C	A	A
PRODUCTS OR SUBSIDIARIES	PayLess Shoe Source			
EXTRAS	Workplace Principles			
NA NA TRADING CO.	A	F	A	A
PRODUCTS OR SUBSIDIARIES	Doc Martens, Na Na shoes, Utility			
EXTRAS	Small company			
NEW BALANCE	I	I	I	F
PRODUCTS OR SUBSIDIARIES	New Balance			

SNEAKERS/SHOES

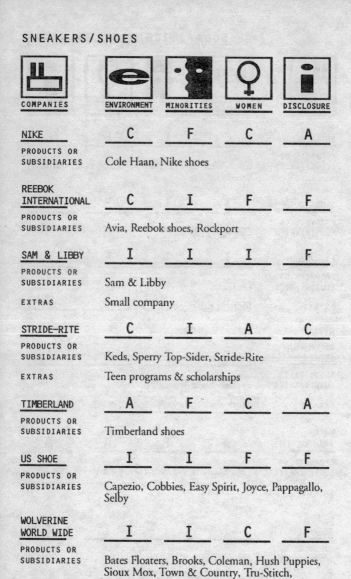

COMPANIES	ENVIRONMENT	MINORITIES	WOMEN	DISCLOSURE
NIKE	C	F	C	A
PRODUCTS OR SUBSIDIARIES	Cole Haan, Nike shoes			
REEBOK INTERNATIONAL	C	I	F	F
PRODUCTS OR SUBSIDIARIES	Avia, Reebok shoes, Rockport			
SAM & LIBBY	I	I	I	F
PRODUCTS OR SUBSIDIARIES	Sam & Libby			
EXTRAS	Small company			
STRIDE-RITE	C	I	A	C
PRODUCTS OR SUBSIDIARIES	Keds, Sperry Top-Sider, Stride-Rite			
EXTRAS	Teen programs & scholarships			
TIMBERLAND	A	F	C	A
PRODUCTS OR SUBSIDIARIES	Timberland shoes			
US SHOE	I	I	F	F
PRODUCTS OR SUBSIDIARIES	Capezio, Cobbies, Easy Spirit, Joyce, Pappagallo, Selby			
WOLVERINE WORLD WIDE	I	I	C	F
PRODUCTS OR SUBSIDIARIES	Bates Floaters, Brooks, Coleman, Hush Puppies, Sioux Mox, Town & Country, Tru-Stitch, Wilderness, Wimzees, Wolverine			

COMPANIES	ENVIRONMENT	MINORITIES	WOMEN	DISCLOSURE
BORDEN	F	A	C	A
PRODUCTS OR SUBSIDIARIES	Borden Juice, Meadow Gold, Thirstee Smash			
EXTRAS	Direct investment in South Africa			
CADBURY SCHWEPPES	A	I	C	A
PRODUCTS OR SUBSIDIARIES	Canada Dry, Crush, Mott's, Schweppes, Sunkist			
EXTRAS	Foreign company			
CAMPBELL SOUP	C	A	A	A
PRODUCTS OR SUBSIDIARIES	La Croix, V8			
EXTRAS	Animal testing: non-medical purposes, significant alternative efforts			
CLOROX	A	A	C	A
PRODUCTS OR SUBSIDIARIES	Deer Park			
EXTRAS	Animal testing: non-medical purposes, significant alternative efforts			
COCA-COLA	C	A	A	A
PRODUCTS OR SUBSIDIARIES	Bright & Early, Coca-Cola, Fanta, Five Alive, Fresca, Hi-C, Mello Yello, Minute Maid, Mr. Pibb, Ramblin' Root Beer, Sprite, Tab			
EXTRAS	Indirect ties to South Africa; Teen programs & scholarships; Workplace Principles			

SODA/JUICE/BOTTLED WATER

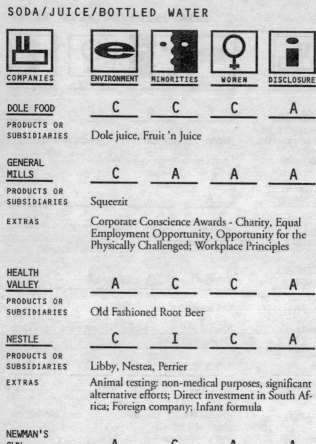

COMPANIES	ENVIRONMENT	MINORITIES	WOMEN	DISCLOSURE
DOLE FOOD	C	C	C	A
PRODUCTS OR SUBSIDIARIES	Dole juice, Fruit 'n Juice			
GENERAL MILLS	C	A	A	A
PRODUCTS OR SUBSIDIARIES	Squeezit			
EXTRAS	Corporate Conscience Awards - Charity, Equal Employment Opportunity, Opportunity for the Physically Challenged; Workplace Principles			
HEALTH VALLEY	A	C	C	A
PRODUCTS OR SUBSIDIARIES	Old Fashioned Root Beer			
NESTLE	C	I	C	A
PRODUCTS OR SUBSIDIARIES	Libby, Nestea, Perrier			
EXTRAS	Animal testing: non-medical purposes, significant alternative efforts; Direct investment in South Africa; Foreign company; Infant formula			
NEWMAN'S OWN	A	C	A	A
PRODUCTS OR SUBSIDIARIES	Newman's lemonade			
EXTRAS	100% profit to charity; Corporate Conscience Award - Charity; Small company			

COMPANIES	ENVIRONMENT	MINORITIES	WOMEN	DISCLOSURE
PEPSICO	C	A	A	A
PRODUCTS OR SUBSIDIARIES	7-UP, Mountain Dew, Mug, Pepsi Cola, Slice			
EXTRAS	Animal testing: non-medical purposes; Factory farming; Indirect ties to South Africa; Teen programs & scholarships			
PHILIP MORRIS	F	A	A	F
PRODUCTS OR SUBSIDIARIES	Country Time, Crystal Light, Kool-Aid, Tang, Wyler's			
EXTRAS	Animal testing: non-medical purposes; Cigarettes; Indirect ties to South Africa; Workplace Principles			
PROCTER & GAMBLE	C	A	C	A
PRODUCTS OR SUBSIDIARIES	Hawaiian Punch, Lincoln, Sunny Delight, Texsun			
EXTRAS	Animal testing: medical and non-medical purposes, significant alternative efforts; Corporate Conscience Awards - Animal Welfare, Employer Responsiveness; Indirect ties to South Africa; Workplace Principles			
QUAKER OATS	C	A	A	A
PRODUCTS OR SUBSIDIARIES	Gatorade			
EXTRAS	Fair Share			

SODA/JUICE/BOTTLED WATER

COMPANIES	ENVIRONMENT	MINORITIES	WOMEN	DISCLOSURE
UNILEVER	C	F	F	A

PRODUCTS OR SUBSIDIARIES: Wyler's

EXTRAS: Animal testing: non-medical purposes, significant alternative efforts; Foreign company

SPORTING GOODS

COMPANIES	ENVIRONMENT	MINORITIES	WOMEN	DISCLOSURE
BRUNSWICK	F	I	C	F

PRODUCTS OR SUBSIDIARIES: Brunswick

EXTRAS: Nuclear weapons

COMPANIES	ENVIRONMENT	MINORITIES	WOMEN	DISCLOSURE
DERBY INTERNATIONAL	I	I	I	F

PRODUCTS OR SUBSIDIARIES: Haro, Nishiki, Raleigh

EXTRAS: Foreign company

COMPANIES	ENVIRONMENT	MINORITIES	WOMEN	DISCLOSURE
HUFFY	C	F	F	A

PRODUCTS OR SUBSIDIARIES: Huffy

COMPANIES	ENVIRONMENT	MINORITIES	WOMEN	DISCLOSURE
LANDS'END	I	I	F	F

PRODUCTS OR SUBSIDIARIES: Lands' End backpacks

COMPANIES	ENVIRONMENT	MINORITIES	WOMEN	DISCLOSURE
PRINCE MANUFACTURING	I	I	I	F

PRODUCTS OR SUBSIDIARIES: Prince

SPORTING GOODS

COMPANIES	ENVIRONMENT	MINORITIES	WOMEN	DISCLOSURE
SPALDING & EVENFLO	I	I	I	F

PRODUCTS OR SUBSIDIARIES Spalding

TAMPONS/SANITARY PADS

COMPANIES	ENVIRONMENT	MINORITIES	WOMEN	DISCLOSURE
JOHNSON & JOHNSON	C	A	A	A

PRODUCTS OR SUBSIDIARIES Carefree, o.b., Stayfree, Sure & Natural

EXTRAS Animal testing: medical purposes only, significant alternative efforts; Direct investment in South Africa; Workplace Principles

COMPANIES	ENVIRONMENT	MINORITIES	WOMEN	DISCLOSURE
KIMBERLY-CLARK	F	A	A	F

PRODUCTS OR SUBSIDIARIES Kotex, Lightdays, New Freedom, Overnites, Security, Simplique, Thin Super, Tru-Fit

EXTRAS Animal testing: non-medical purposes

COMPANIES	ENVIRONMENT	MINORITIES	WOMEN	DISCLOSURE
PLAYTEX FP GROUP	I	I	I	F

PRODUCTS OR SUBSIDIARIES Playtex, Ultimates

EXTRAS Animal testing: non-medical purposes

TAMPONS/SANITARY PADS

COMPANIES	ENVIRONMENT	MINORITIES	WOMEN	DISCLOSURE
PROCTER & GAMBLE	C	A	C	A
SEVENTH GENERATION	A	C	A	A
TAMBRANDS	A	I	C	C

PROCTER & GAMBLE

PRODUCTS OR SUBSIDIARIES: Always

EXTRAS: Animal testing: medical and non-medical purposes, significant alternative efforts; Corporate Conscience Awards - Animal Welfare, Employer Responsiveness; Indirect ties to South Africa; Workplace Principles

SEVENTH GENERATION

PRODUCTS OR SUBSIDIARIES: Seventh Generation sanitary pads

EXTRAS: CERES Principles; Small company

TAMBRANDS

PRODUCTS OR SUBSIDIARIES: Tampax

EXTRAS: Indirect ties to South Africa

CHAPTER 10

Shopping for your future

Top Teen Brands

SHOPPING FOR YOUR FUTURE: TOP TEEN BRANDS

THE LOWDOWN ON THOSE UPTOWN BRANDS

Now that you've had a chance to read the ratings chapters, we thought you'd like to know more about some of the companies that make brands teens buy most—a sort of behind-the-scenes look at ratings. For these 11 companies, we've dug up nuggets of information out of our piles of research materials. Some are good, some are not so good, and some are terrible. There should have been 12 companies in this section. But after scouring our files, trying to talk to the company, and asking our advisers for help, we could not find any reliable information on Helene Curtis (Suave and Salon Selectives shampoos).

Reading this chapter, you'll see how complicated it can be to decide whether to support a company—or not. Does Levi's model policy on employees with AIDS outweigh its laying off low-income, Hispanic workers in Texas? Does McDonald's switching from styrofoam to paper mean it's now environmentally okay? If The Gap has some terrific environmental programs—but won't tell us anything about it—how should we rate it? In this chapter, we leave it to you to decide according to your own values. You be the judge.

COCA-COLA

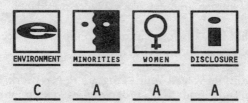

ENVIRONMENT	MINORITIES	WOMEN	DISCLOSURE
C	A	A	A

EXTRAS Indirect ties to South Africa; Teen programs & scholarships; Workplace Principles

- Coca-Cola and its other brands—Sprite, Tab, Fresca, Fanta—are sold in 185 countries, including South Africa and the Commonwealth of Independent States (the former Soviet Union).

- Coke plans to spend $1 billion over the next four years with minority and women suppliers. According to the president of the National Minority Development Council, "About 30 companies are the heart and soul of minority supply in the U.S. and Coca-Cola is one of them."

- 10.9% of the company's 10,250 employees are black. 3.9% of all senior managers and 5.5% of the company's corporate officers are black.

- In 1992, Coke was listed in ***Hispanic*** magazine as one of the top 100 companies for Hispanic opportunity.

- Coke was included in a 1992 ***Black Enterprise*** article called "25 Best Places for Blacks to Work" for its training and development programs and its Diversity Task Force, which encourages a multiculture world.

- Women hold high-level positions in the company: One woman is on the 14-member board of directors and there are two women among Coke's 22 vice presidents.

- Coke has fully disclosed information to CEP since our first shopping guide in 1987.

- Coke runs its Valued Youth Program in New York, California, and Florida. This program tries to keep "at risk" students from dropping out of school by sponsoring tutors in middle and elementary schools.

The largest soft drink company in the world, Coca-Cola is strong in minority and women's advancement.

THE GAP

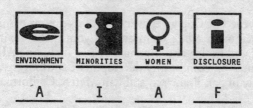

ENVIRONMENT	MINORITIES	WOMEN	DISCLOSURE
A	I	A	F

- The Gap Inc. owns 800 Gap stores, 155 Banana Republics, 245 GapKids, seven Gap shoe stores and a Baby Gap across the U.S., Canada, and Europe. In 1991, Gap clothes became the second-largest-selling brand name in the United States. (The largest is Coca-Cola.)

- The Gap's sales in 1991 were over $2.5 billion; sales grew 83% during the first six months of 1991. The company has 37,000 employees.

- The Gap is in an industry criticized for its damaging environmental impact from stonewashing and unsustainable use of cotton.

- The Gap has switched to recycled papers and packaging. Gap shopping bags are recycled paper with over 10% post-consumer fiber by weight and are no longer clay-coated, making them easier to recycle. Hang tags and "flashers"—the tags stitched to jeans pockets—will be printed on recycled stock. The wooden pallets at distribution centers are being replaced with recycled plastic pallets, which last 20 years instead of six months.

- Although these changes have a positive environmental impact, they also save the company money.

- The company will not talk to anyone on the outside. The Gap calls this "not politicizing the clothes." Just because the company wouldn't tell us anything does not necessarily mean it is socially irresponsible. But for a company this big to keep secrets is irresponsible.

- Each year The Gap gives away 1% of its pre-tax earnings in three main areas: children and youth, the environment, and health and human services, including AIDS. It focuses on community development and poverty, especially in San Francisco and San Mateo, California.

- The company has a program to match the gifts of any employee to a nonprofit organization or school. Employees are given up to five paid hours per month to volunteer at the organization of their choice.

The Gap Inc., the country's largest clothing retailer, refused to disclose information to CEP.

GRAND METROPOLITAN

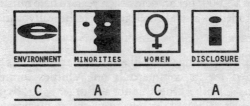

ENVIRONMENT	MINORITIES	WOMEN	DISCLOSURE
C	A	C	A

EXTRAS — Factory farming; Foreign company; Teen programs & scholarships

- Burger King has switched to what it calls "earthhappy" packaging. Plain paper wrappings and bags made from recycled newsprint replaced plastic-coated paper sandwich boxes and sacks made with bleached paper. The company says this will cut down on trash by about 15,000 tons a year.

- Like most fast-food companies, Burger King gets its meat from factory farms.

- In 1990, Burger King's slogan "sometimes you've gotta break the rules" took on a new meaning. The U.S. Labor Department charged certain restaurants with child labor law abuses, mostly for violating hour and age restrictions. The company admitted to "an unacceptable record of violations" of child labor rules since 1986, faced $318,000 in fines, and said it was committed to dealing with the problem.

- The multimillion-dollar Burger King Academy Program reaches out to kids who have dropped out or who are not doing well in school. In partnership with the Department of Justice and Cities In Schools, Inc., the Burger King Corporation has set up 27 private, alternative high schools. Students not only learn basic academics, they get on-site counseling and help such as child care.

• The company's Academy Scholarship Program awards one $3,000 scholarship and two $1,000 scholarships (a total of $5,000) per academy each year, to help outstanding students attend college or technical/vocational school.

• Burger King, along with Nike and some others, has been criticized for its commercials on Whittle Communications' Channel One. But not all Burger King ads pitch a product. Created by award-winning documentary filmmakers, some spots illustrate the problems of dropping out and show young people struggling with early pregnancy, drugs, and crime. Burger King's name and logo appears just once.

Burger King is owned by London-based Grand Metropolitan, an international food, beverage, and retailing company that gets about 30% of its income from the sale of alcoholic drinks.

LEVI STRAUSS

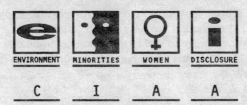

ENVIRONMENT	MINORITIES	WOMEN	DISCLOSURE
C	I	A	A

EXTRAS Workplace Principles

- Levi Strauss is the largest clothing company in the world, with 1991 sales of close to $5 billion of jeans, Dockers, and other casual wear in 70 countries. It has 23,000 employees in the U.S. and 8,500 employees abroad.

- Levi has come up with a way to stop using bleach and dyes on some kinds of jeans: cotton that grows naturally in brown or green.

- The company estimates that 90–100% of its total packaging is made of recycled materials.

- Levi, along with many American garment companies, has been criticized for closing plants and firing workers. Levi closed 26 plants between 1985 and 1990. About 6,000 workers lost their jobs.

- In 1990 Levi closed a plant in San Antonio, Texas and moved to Central America. Many of the 1,115, mostly Latino, San Antonio workers had little education or other job skills. Levi did provide more severance benefits than the law requires, but an organization called Fuerza Unida was formed to fight for more help. Laid-off workers were especially worried about medical costs for job-related injuries. Fuerza Unida called for a boycott of

Levi's products and sued the company. This boycott is still active.

- Labor groups have criticized Levi for possible exploitation of the overseas workers that produce its products. The average wage in the Dominican Republic or Costa Rica is $1 an hour, while American workers earn $6–7 per hour.

- Yet the company is unusual in having a specific policy, which covers the environment and child labor for its 400 overseas contractors. These strict guidelines are evidence that Levi is trying to act responsibly.

- Levi has helped people with AIDS since 1982. It bans discrimination against workers with the disease and has expanded its usual insurance coverage with home health care and hospice care. Levi tries to adapt schedules that allow infected employees to continue work.

- In 1992, Levi became the largest American company to cover employees' unmarried partners in its health plan. This policy includes both heterosexual and homosexual couples.

- Also in 1992, Levi stopped funding the Boy Scouts. The company said that it will not fund an organization that discriminates against homosexuals, who are not allowed to become scoutmasters.

Although Levi Strauss has been criticized for its practices in some areas, it takes its social responsibility seriously.

MCDONALD'S

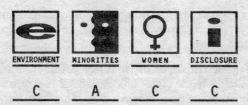

ENVIRONMENT	MINORITIES	WOMEN	DISCLOSURE
C	A	C	C

EXTRAS Factory farming; Fair Share; Teen programs & scholarships

- McDonald's is the largest foodservice organization in the world, with over 12,400 restaurants in 59 countries, including South Korea, Yugoslavia, Hungary, and Cuba.

- McDonald's is the largest consumer of beef in the world, using 1% of all beef produced in the United States. Most, if not all, of this beef comes from "factory farms," which have been criticized as cruel to animals.

- The 85 billion hamburgers McDonald's has sold took 36 million cows, 85 trillion gallons of water to grow their feed, and released 14.4 million tons of methane, a greenhouse gas.

- For every quarter-pound of hamburger exported from the South American rainforest region, 55 square feet of rainforest is destroyed.

- McDonald's used styrofoam packaging until 1990, when consumer pressure, much of it from kids, convinced the company to switch to plastic-coated paper. The company had defended styrofoam for several years, although it is not biodegradable and its production releases chemicals that damage the ozone layer.

- *Black Enterprise* magazine named McDonald's one of its "25 Best Places for Blacks to Work" for reviewing managers' performance on equal opportunity issues and helping employees develop careers. 13.2% of senior management at the company is black.

- Nearly 70% of McDonald's restaurant management and 25% of the company's executives are minorities and women.

- The largest employer of minority youth in America, McDonald's is the target of a Philadelphia group's boycott because studies showed that inner-city fast-food workers were making up to $1 an hour less than suburban workers.

- The company did not answer CEP's social responsibility questionnaire, but it does devote a section of its annual report to social issues. McDonald's printed its 1991 annual report on recycled newspaper with a reduced amount of paper.

- McDonald's employs the mentally and physically impaired through its McJobs program. McPride helps keep students in school by rewarding them for academic achievement.

- After the 1992 Los Angeles riots, McDonald's showed heart in the inner-city by feeding fire fighters, police and national guard troops as well as local residents and 300 elementary school students free of charge.

- The company supports 153 Ronald McDonald Houses where families of seriously ill children can stay for a small fee or no fee while the child is undergoing extensive medical treatment.

McDonald's has a pretty strong social responsibility record, but there are a few clouds over those golden arches.

NIKE

ENVIRONMENT	MINORITIES	WOMEN	DISCLOSURE
C	F	C	A

- Nike had sales of more than $3 billion in 1991 when its sneakers retook the sales lead from Reebok. The company also sells expensive, Italian leather shoes (under Cole-Haan) and athletic wear. Plus it has 40 retail stores across the country.

- Nike will soon make shoes with outsoles made of waste from its production process. The company plans to use ground-up shoes to make the outsoles, so old sneakers will not end up in landfills.

- Nike has reduced its hazardous waste by nearly 50% since 1990, and it recycles paper, corrugated cardboard, glass, plastic, cans, and toner cartridges at its headquarters. All locations recycle paper. Nike also stopped using CFCs, ozone-depleting gases, in its manufacturing processes.

- Operation PUSH, a civil rights group, called for a boycott of Nike in 1990. The group said that, although Nike sells 30% to blacks, it does not have many blacks in leadership positions and does not return enough to the black community. PUSH singled out Nike because it receives more than half the money spent by blacks on athletic shoes.

- Nike appointed John Thompson, the Georgetown University basketball coach, to its board, and has set affirmative action goals for all minorities.

- Nike now has above-average company programs to advance both members of minority groups and women. It also uses minority-owned banks in areas where it has retail stores or other operations.

- Rap group Public Enemy sings about Nike not supporting the community: "I like Nike/But wait a minute/The neighborhood supports, so put some money in it."

- 99% of Nike shoes are made in Asia, about half in South Korea and the rest split among Indonesia, China, Thailand, and Taiwan. By shifting manufacturing to these countries, Nike holds the cost of making $130 Air Jordans (which wholesale for $68.75) to just $30.

- Nike has been criticized for its manufacturing policies overseas, especially in Indonesia. The minimum wage there is below the government's idea of the minimum necessary to survive. Many of Nike's competitors also manufacture shoes in these areas.

- The company offers strong family benefits, including day care at its headquarters.

- Nike funds Just Do It drop-out prevention grants, which are administered by the National Foundation for the Improvement of Education. The program began in 1991 and is scheduled to give out $1 million over three years. Each year, 20 grants go to about 60 teachers with drop-out prevention proposals. Many of the programs funded by Nike end up being adopted by the school districts or local businesses.

Nike rates better in the environment and women than it does on minorities. It cooperated fully with CEP and completed the entire questionnaire.

PEPSICO

ENVIRONMENT	MINORITIES	WOMEN	DISCLOSURE
C	A	A	A

EXTRAS — Animal testing: non-medical purposes; Factory farming; Indirect ties to South Africa; Teen programs & scholarships

- Pepsi Cola is the number two cola next to Coke. It also owns 7-Up, Slice, Mountain Dew, Frito-Lay, and Doritos Snack Foods. Its market value is $20 billion.

- PepsiCo owns more restaurants, including Kentucky Fried Chicken, Pizza Hut, and Taco Bell, than any other company in the world.

- Although the Food and Drug Administration requires Pepsi test new ingredients on animals, the company tries to avoid repeating tests by working with others in the same business and sharing test results.

- PepsiCo was listed among the "Top 25 Places for Blacks to Work" in *Black Enterprise* magazine for its mentoring programs, recruitment efforts at minority colleges, its Black Employees Association, and its purchasing from minority vendors. Of 24,432 domestic employees, 12% are black.

- Pepsi was rated in *Hispanic* magazine as one of the 100 U.S. companies that provide the best opportunities for Hispanics.

- A high 30% of officials and managers are women.

- Pepsi has given CEP thorough information on its social impact since 1991.

- The PepsiCo Foundation for Higher Education spends more than $3 million a year for 15 college and university projects. Since 1989 The Pepsi School Challenge has kept Dallas and Detroit inner-city high-school students in school by awarding each graduating student a $500 credit for every year of school successfully completed.

- Pepsi After School Spots provide inner-city elementary children with safe after-school hang-outs in cities such as Savannah, Georgia and Gainesville and Jacksonville, Florida.

- Pepsi has been boycotted since it decided to keep operating its Rangoon, Burma bottling plant. Burma's military regime is considered one of the most oppressive governments in the world—and it owns 60% of the plant.

PepsiCo really reaches out to minority communities.

PROCTER & GAMBLE

ENVIRONMENT	MINORITIES	WOMEN	DISCLOSURE
C	A	C	A

EXTRA — Animal testing: medical and non-medical purposes, significant alternative efforts; Corporate Conscience Awards - Animal Welfare, Employer Responsiveness; Indirect ties to South Africa; Workplace Principles

- P&G has tried to improve its environmental record. It uses refillable cartons for laundry concentrates and asks its suppliers to use recycled plastic in making bottles for many of its products. But some of those products themselves are bad for the environment.

- People who live in Florida's Taylor County filed a lawsuit against P&G, claiming the company's cellulose plant has polluted their drinking water. P&G dumps 50 million gallons of effluent a day into the Fenholloway River—all legal because of a 1947 Florida law.

- During hearings on a bill to require recycled content and limits on "green" marketing claims, P&G would not support voluntary industry guidelines or state legislation.

- P&G has reduced its use of animals for testing 52% since 1984. The company has developed new tests that are more humane and use far fewer animals. It spent more than $14 million between 1986 and 1990 on new testing methods.

- In 1989 a P&G memo, not meant for the public, was leaked. It suggested forming a national group to promote the "judicious use of animal testing." The company met with animal rights organizations to assure them that its intent was to make clear the company's belief that limited animal testing is necessary until alternative methods have been approved.

- Three out of 125 corporate officers are members of minority groups, one of whom is among the 25 highest paid; one minority serves on the 19-member board.

- The Sycamore Investment Company, a P&G subsidiary, lends money to help minorities start and expand businesses.

- Five of the 125 corporate officers are women and one serves on the board. Although 15% of college engineering grads are women and 10% minorities, P&G's technical divisions' new hires are more than 40% women and 20% minorities.

- The company helped fund four childcare centers used by employees.

- Benefits include eight weeks' paid leave and up to one year unpaid leave after childbirth plus $2,000 for employees adopting a child.

- P&G still has a profit-sharing plan begun in 1887—the first one ever in the U.S.!

Overall, ratings are good, but Procter & Gamble has sent mixed messages on the environment.

REEBOK

ENVIRONMENT	MINORITIES	WOMEN	DISCLOSURE
C	I	F	F

- Reebok International Ltd. sells footwear and athletic clothes in more than 40 countries. After several years at the top of the U.S. market, it now ranks second to Nike.

- 90% of Reebok cartons and tissues are made of recycled paper.

- The company is trying to figure out a way to recycle discarded shoes into a new product.

- In 1990 Reebok Chairman Paul Fireman was on the national committee that helped to raise $8 million for anti-apartheid leader Nelson Mandela's eight-city tour of America.

- The Reebok Foundation, which tries to promote "individual freedom and social change," was one of the sponsors of the 1990 Boston Walk of Freedom. Thousands of high school and college students walked two miles to raise funds for black South African teenagers' training and education.

- Reebok has expanded its advertising in minority-owned media, makes deposits in minority banks, and uses minority professional services.

- Only one woman is among Reebok's eight top corporate officers and the board of directors has none.

- Reebok did not respond to CEP's social responsibility questionnaire.

- Reebok, along with many shoe companies, is criticized by several watchdog groups for using factories that have low wages and bad working conditions in the Far East. Half of its manufacturing is done in South Korea, with the rest in Thailand, China, and Indonesia.

- The Reebok Human Rights Award is presented annually to honor people under 30 "who, against great odds and often at personal risk, have advanced the cause of human rights."

- Reebok is a charter member of Businesses for Social Responsibility, which supports stricter environmental and safety regulations as well as investment in a variety of health, education, and welfare programs. The group also wants to help develop inner-city businesses.

Reebok is a corporate social leader in the area of human rights. Unfortunately, its track record in some other social issues is less impressive.

SONY

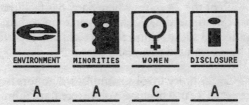

ENVIRONMENT	MINORITIES	WOMEN	DISCLOSURE
A	A	C	A

EXTRAS Fair Share; Foreign company; Teen programs & scholarships

- Sony was first with Walkman radios, audio cassette players, and compact disc players. The company also makes videotapes, movies, and owns Columbia and Epic CD and record labels.

- The company has stopped using freon (an environmental threat) to make videotape. It is also planning smaller cases for audiotapes to reduce waste plastic.

- An 11-member recycling team at Sony Magnetic Products, Inc. supervises recycling of plastic, metal, wood, aluminum, oil and other materials. One result: nearly all motor and lubricating oils used at this facility are recycled.

- The company works with the John Conti Rehabilitation Center in Alabama to run a plastic cassette recycling center.

- Sony has a scholarship program at high schools in Dothan, Alabama, and Escondido, California. Kids with a 3.0 or better grade point average, good attendance, and involvement in school and community activities are eligible. Final winners receive up to $2,500 per year for four years toward their college education.

- Sony celebrated its 30th anniversary in the U.S. with the Sony Student Project Abroad. Two high school students from each of the 24 states where Sony has facilities took a two-week trip in the U.S. and Japan to introduce them to a variety of social, cultural, and technical experiences. Sony has continued this yearly event.

- Sony's Community Involvement Award honors five employees each year who have volunteered at community organizations. Sony contributes $1,000 to the nonprofit organizations where the winners volunteer.

In 1972 Sony became the first Japanese manufacturer to establish a plant in the U.S. It works hard to get involved in American communities and to help young Americans learn more about Japanese culture and customs.

TIME WARNER

ENVIRONMENT	MINORITIES	WOMEN	DISCLOSURE
C	A	A	A

- On March 4, 1989, Time Inc. and Warner Communications Inc. merged to form one company, now the world's largest media and entertainment empire. It combines Time's print and cable TV businesses with Warner's music, movie and TV companies, and its own publishing divisions. The company now owns Warner Bros. Records; Warner Bros. Television and Movies; DC comics, publisher of Batman, Superman, and Wonder Woman; Mad magazine; HBO; Time, People, Sports Illustrated, and Fortune; and many more.

- The merger between Time and Warner has been criticized as creating a media giant that has too much power over the flow of information to the public. The whole media industry has gotten more and more concentrated in a few large conglomerates.

- Time Warner came up with the Eco-Pak for compact discs as an alternative to the longbox. The Eco-Pak container is made entirely of recycled paperboard and plastic. It generates no waste other than the shrink-wrap in which it is delivered.

- Time Warner owns 37% of Whittle Communications, the producer of Channel One television for schools. Whittle plans a chain of private, for-profit schools, called the Edison Project. Should the largest media company in the world have that much influence over young people's education?

- The company not only completed CEP's social responsibility questionnaire, it even publishes its own social responsibility report, called "Making a Difference."

- Time Warner won CEP's Corporate Conscience Award in 1991, in the category of Community Action. Since 1935, Time has been committed to education and the fight against illiteracy through cheap student subscriptions, instructional materials, and adopt-a-school programs.

- The company also tells employees about volunteer opportunities through a bimonthly newsletter.

- Time Warner offers a good range of programs to help employees balance work and family. There is a company-sponsored center for children whose usual arrangements fall through. Time Warner is one of a 15-company group that provides emergency at-home care, for times when a child is mildly sick or the usual babysitter does not show.

- Warner artist Ice-T's song "Cop Killer" caused a lot of controversy last year. Law enforcement officials called for a boycott of Time Warner, criticizing the song for encouraging people to attack police officers. Time Warner stood by the song and the freedom of artists to say what they like. But after Ice-T asked them to remove it from the album, they did.

- Time Warner has been criticized for excessive pay to its highest officers. In 1990, Chairman and co-Chief Executive Officer Steve Ross made $78.2 million, $74.9 million of which was a one-time payment from the Time buyout of Warner. Critics complained that the total amount was the largest among executives of public companies, and more than twice the combined salaries of 605 Time Warner employees laid off that year.

Time Warner has a strong commitment to the community and is willing to talk about its social responsibility record.

CHAPTER 11

It's in your hands

IT'S IN YOUR HANDS

BOOKS

50 Simple Things Kids Can Do To Save The Earth
Earthworks Group, (Andrews and McMeel, 1990). Aimed at 8–14-year-olds.

The 100 Best Companies to Work for in America
Robert Levering and Milton Moskowitz, (Doubleday, 1993). A look at companies through the eyes of their employees.

Facing Our Future: From Denial to Environmental Action
Jim Cole, (Growing Images, 1991). An upbeat look at how to help the earth.

Good Works
Jessica Cowan, (Barricade Books, 1991). A guide to careers in social change.

The Kid's Guide to Social Action
Barbara Lewis, (Free Spirit, 1991). How to solve problems in many different areas, from homelessness to racial prejudice. Includes sample press releases, letters to legislators, survey forms, petitions, proposals, grant applications, and lots more.

Kid Heroes of the Environment
Earthworks Group, (Earthworks Press, 1991). Short stories about young people who've helped the environment.

Save The Earth: An Action Handbook for Kids
Betty Miles, (Alfred Knopf, 1991). More ideas on how kids can help save the environment.

Shopping for a Better World 1992
Council on Economic Priorities, (Ballantine Books, 1992). The original guide to corporate social responsibility with ratings on almost 200 companies.

Shopping Guide for Caring Consumers: A Guide to Products That Are Not Tested On Animals
People for the Ethical Treatment of Animals, (The Book Publishing Company, 1993). List of 400 cruelty-free companies.

MAGAZINES, NEWSLETTERS, AND OTHER PUBLICATIONS

Community Jobs: The Employment Newspaper for the Non-Profit Sector
50 Beacon St.
Boston, MA 02108
Lists both paid and volunteer internships with socially responsible organizations.

Consumer Reports
101 Truman Ave.
Yonkers, NY 10703
Rates products for quality and cost.

Co-op America Quarterly
1850 M St., NW
Washington, DC 20036
Helps consumers and investors "vote with their dollars." Includes Boycott Action News.

Dollars & Sense
One Summer St.
Somerville, MA 02143
Economics from an alternative, liberal angle. Special student subscription rates.

Garbage
P.O. Box 51647
Boulder, CO 80321
A practical approach to the environment.

Greenpeace Magazine
1436 U St.
Washington, DC 20009
(202)462-1177
An accessible adult environmental publication.

Ms.
230 Park Ave.
New York, NY 10169
The original feminist magazine.

P-3
P.O. Box 52
Montgomery, VT 05470
Devoted to the third planet, earth, and geared to kids.

Sierra
730 Polk St.
San Francisco, CA 94109
The magazine of the Sierra Club.

Student Network News (Humane Society of USA)
67 Salem Rd.
East Haddam, CT 06423
(203)434-8666
A newsletter about animal welfare for high school students.

Wall St. Journal Classroom Edition
P.O. Box 7019
Chicopee, MA 01021
1-800-628-9320
Special high school version of the financial newspaper.

Zillions
P.O. Box 54861
Boulder, CO 80322
Consumer Reports for 8-14 year-olds.

ORGANIZATIONS: ADVERTISING

Center for Media and Values

1962 S. Shenandoah St.
Los Angeles, CA 90034
(310)559-2944
An anti-commercialism group that puts out Media and Values magazine.

Center for the Study of Commercialism

1875 Connecticut Ave. NW
Washington, DC 20009
(202)797-7080
This new group exposes and opposes commercialism through a quarterly newsletter.

Mail Preference Service

c/o Direct Marketing Assn.
11 W. 42nd St.
New York, NY 10163
They'll get your name off junk mail lists.

The Media Foundation

1243 W. 7th Ave.
Vancouver, British Columbia
V6H IB7 Canada
(604)736-9401
They publish Adbusters Quarterly magazine, criticize ad campaigns, promote media awareness.

Smokefree Educational Services Inc.

375 South End Ave. #32F
New York, NY 10280
An anti-smoking organization, it sponsors a kids' poster campaign, a book, and posters.

STAT: Stop Teenage Addiction to Tobacco

121 Lyman St. #210
Springfield, MA 01103
Newsletter, Tobacco and Youth Reporter, posters, books, T-shirts, speakers.

ORGANIZATIONS: CHILDREN'S RIGHTS AND POLICY

The Children's Defense Fund

25 E St. NW
Washington, DC 20001
(202)628-8787
An educational, lobbying group that pays particular attention to needs of poor, minority, and disabled children.

Children's Rights Project

132 W. 43rd St. 6th Floor
New York, NY 10036
(212)944-9800
Concerned with litigation, education, and public policy issues affecting families and children.

ORGANIZATIONS: ENVIRONMENTAL/ANIMAL WELFARE

Environmental Defense Fund
257 Park Ave. South
New York, NY 10010
(800)CALL EDF
They have a recycling information service.

Friends of the Earth
218 D St.
Washington, DC 20003
(202)544-2600
Global environmental advocates.

Greenpeace
1436 U St.
Washington, DC 20009
(202)462-1177
One of the most activist-oriented environmental groups.

Green Seal
1250 23rd St., NW #275
Washington, DC 20037
(202)331-7337
They give a seal of approval to products that meet environmental standards.

Humane Society of the United States
2100 L St.
Washington, DC 20037
(202)452-1100
A moderate animal welfare organization.

Kids Against Pollution
275 High St.
Closter, NJ 07624
(201)768-1332
A small membership fee gets you a packet of information on how to fight pollution.

Kids for a Clean Environment
P.O. Box 158254
Nashville, TN 37215
This free, nation-wide club has a newsletter.

People for the Ethical Treatment of Animals
P.O. Box 42516
Washington, DC 20015
(301)770-7444
A radical animal rights group.

Sierra Club
730 Polk St.
San Francisco, CA 94109
(415)776-2211
One of the country's biggest environmental lobbyists.

Student Environmental Action Coalition
P.O. Box 1168
Chapel Hill, NC 27514
40,000 members on 1,500 college and high school campuses hold conferences, meet with corporate heads, and spread the word.

Worldwatch Institute
1776 Massachusetts Ave.
Washington, DC 20036
(202)452-1999
A research group that monitors the whole earth.

Youth for Environmental Sanity
607 Frederick St.
Santa Cruz, CA 95062
(408)459-9344
The YES! group tours the country with assemblies.

ORGANIZATIONS: CAREER/FINANCES

Career Works
P.O. Box 316
Norwich, VT 05055
(802) 649-5650
An employment agency for socially responsible jobs.

Good Work!
619 G St.
Arcata, CA 95521
(707)826-7033
These folks will come speak to groups on how to have careers that match your values. They also are coming out with a book on the subject.

High School Financial Planning Program
College for Financial Planning
4695 South Monaco St.
Denver, CO 80237
(303) 220-1200
A complete course in how to budget your money, free to teachers.

The Larger Context: Center for the Advancement of Socially Responsible Careers
P.O. Box 3242
Burlington, VT 05401
They offer conferences and workshops on this subject.

New Roadmap Foundation
P.O. Box 15981
Seattle, WA 98115
(206)527-0437
A group devoted to living as cheaply as possible in order to escape having to have regular jobs. Members then spend their time in volunteer or creative work. They have a book on how to achieve financial independence.

ORGANIZATIONS: FOR A BETTER WORLD

Catalyst
250 Park Ave. South
New York, NY 10003
(212)777-8900
Works with businesses on women's advancement through research and advisory services.

The Giraffe Project
197 Second St.
Langley, WA 98260
(206)221-7989
Singles out individuals who've stuck their necks out to make the world a better place. A newsletter profiles these "giraffes."

National Association for the Advancement of Colored People
Youth and College Division
4805 Mt. Hope Dr.
Baltimore, MD 21215
(301)358-8900, ext. 9142

National Organization for Women
1000 16th St.
Washington, DC 20036
(202)331-0066

Young and Teen Peacemakers
37 Lebanon St.
Hamilton, NY 13346
(315)824-4332
A newsletter about how to work toward world peace.

U.S. Public Interest Research Group
215 Pennsylvania Ave. SE
Washington, DC 20003
They do research and fight for consumer and environmental protection.

CREDIT CARDS

America's Black Colleges
(800)343-4300

Child Welfare League of America
(202)638-2952

COOP America
(800)424-2667

Defenders of Wildlife
(800)972-9979

Sierra Club
(415) 776-2211

Working Assets
(800)522-7759

HIGH SCHOOL CREDIT UNIONS

Alternatives FCU
301 State St.
Ithaca, NY 14850
(607)273-4611

Big Island Educational FCU
66 Lono St.
Hilo, HI 96720
(808)935-9778

Brockton CU
68 Legion Pkwy.
Brockton, MA 02401
(617)586-2080

Bur Bank FCU
1715 W. Magnolia Blvd.
Burbank, CA 91516
(818)846-5143

Cathedral CU Cooperative Society
Port of Spain
Trinidad, West Indies
(809)623-0317

Community FCU
500 S. Harvey St.
Plymouth, MI 48170
(313)453-1200

Edwards Wells FCU
786 State St.
Springfield, MA 01109

Eastern CU Student/Youth Facility
Bushe St. Southern Main Rd.
Curepe, Trinidad
(809)663-2309

Gardner Franco-American FCU
P.O. Box 468
Gardner, MA 01440
(617)632-6200

Granite District CU
441 E. 3900 St.
Salt Lake City, UT 84107
(801)262-6424

H-F FCU
999 Kedzie
Flossmoor, IL 60422
(312)957-1991

I-C CU
300 Bemis Rd.
Fitchburg, MA 01420
(617)343-3726

Leominster Credit Union
20 Adams St.
Leominster, MA 01453

Lowry Federal Credit Union
4000 E. Quincy Ave.
Englewood, CO 80110
(303)770-7660

Oahu One CU
2219 Pauea Rd.
Honolulu, HI 96813
(808)521-6727

Potlatch No. 1 FCU
3113 E. Main
Lewiston, ID 83501
(208)743-1591

Regional FCU
7144 Kennedy Ave.
Hammond, IN 46323
(219)762-2930

Riverside County Schools CU
P.O. Box 908
Riverside, CA 92502
(714)636-8304

Rockland CU
241 Union St.
Rockland, MA 02370
(617)878-0232

Saugus CU
448 Lincoln Ave.
Saugus, MA 01906
(617)233-0010

Southbridge CU
205 Main St.
Southbridge, MA 01550

St. Mary's Credit Union
133 W. Main St.
Marlborough, MA 01752

Warren Schools CU
7277 Bernice
Center Line, MI 48015
(313)755-3800

COLLEGE CREDIT UNIONS

Babson Student FCU
Babson College
P.O. Box 2613
Babson Park, MA 02157
(617)239-4394

CAL Berkeley FCU
University of California, Berkeley
P.O. Box 4000 F
Berkeley, CA 94704
(510)540-6636

Carolina Students CU
Franklin Graham Student Center
P.O. Box 34
Chapel Hill, NC 27514
(919)942-5919

First Ohio Student FCU
305 Baker Center
Athens, OH 45701

Fordham FCU
Fordham University
P.O. Box 618
Bronx, NY 10458
(212)579-2620

Georgetown University Student FCU
Georgetown University
P.O. Box 2299
Washington, DC 20057
(202)625-8560

Georgia Tech FCU
Student Center, Georgia Tech
P.O. Box 36696
Atlanta, GA 30332
(404)875-4204

Howard University Student FCU
2601 16th St. NW
Washington, DC 20009
(202)387-2856

Illini Student FCU
1001 S. Wright St.
Champaign, IL 61820
(217)328-7283

MiamiUniversity Student FCU
208 Warfield Hall
Oxford, OH 45056

Missouri Student FCU
University of Missouri
230 Brady Commons
Columbia, MO 65211
(314)443-8462

Old Queens Student FCU
Rutgers Student Center
New Brunswick, NJ 08903
(201)745-0072

Purdue Student FCU
Stewart Center
P.O. Box 673
West Lafayette, IN 47906
(317)743-0285

Skidmore Students FCU
Skidmore College
Saratoga Springs, NY 12866
(518)584-5000

University of Pennsylvania FCU
3417 Spruce St.
Philadelphia, PA 19104
(215)898-9442

UCB Student FCU
University of Colorado, Boulder
P.O. Box 207
Boulder, CO 80309
(303)492-5519

UCONN Student FCU
University of Connecticut
P.O. Box U-8
Storrs, CT 06268
(203)429-1393

UMASS Student FCU
University of Massachusetts
314 Student Union
Amherst, MA 01003
(413)545-2800

UMO Student FCU
University of Maine
Orono, ME 04473
(207)581-1770

UCSD Student CU
UC San Diego
La Jolla, CA 92093
(619)459-7495

University & State FCU
10045 Mesa Rim Rd.
San Diego, CA 92121
(619)697-1601

University Student FCU
University of Chicago
5706 S. University
Chicago, IL 60637
(312)324-6354

University of Louisville
Student Center
Louisville, KY 40292
(502)588-7321

Washington Square Student FCU
San Jose State University
P.O. Box 4814
San Jose, CA 95150
(408)947-7273

Western's CU Inc.
181 White St.
Danbury, CT 06810
(203)797-4274

Westwood Student FCU
UCLA
P.O. Box 261
Los Angeles, CA 90024
(213)825-1211

STATE LABOR DEPARTMENTS

State Programs Division
Alabama Dept. of Industrial Relations
AL
205-242-8265

Labor Standards and Safety Division
Alaska State Dept. of Labor
AK
907-269-4900

Industrial Commission of Arizona
Arizona State Labor Dept.
AZ
602-542-5887

Labor Standards
Arkansas State Dept. of Labor
AR
501-682-4501

Child Labor Law
Board of Education
DC
202-576-6942

Division of Labor Standards Enforcement
California State Dept. of Labor
CA
415-703-4750

Division of Labor
Colorado State Dept. of Labor
CO
303-894-7530

OSHA/Working Conditions Division
Connecticut State Dept. of Labor
CT
203-566-4550

Administrator of Labor Law Enforcement
64 State Office Building
DE
302-577-2882

Dept. of Labor and Employment Security
Florida State Dept. of Labor
FL
904-488-3131

Industrial Safety Unit
Georgia State Department of Labor
GA
404-656-3613

OSHA
Guam Dept. of Labor
GU
671-646-9321

Dept. of Labor and Industrial Relations
Hawaii State Department of Labor
HI
808-548-7623

ESA Wage and Hour Division
Idaho State Department of Labor
ID
208-334-3950

Child Labor
Illinois State Department of Labor
IL
312-793-2804

Bureau of Child Labor
Indiana State Department of Labor
IN
317-232-2675

Child/Migrant Labor Section
Iowa Division of Labor
IA
515-281-7028

Employment Standards
Kansas Division of Employment
KS
913-296-4062

Div. of Employment Standards & Mediation
Kentucky Labor Cabinet
KY
502-564-2784

Minors Section
Louisiana Office of Labor
LA
504-342-7824

Wage and Hour Division
Maine State Department of Labor
ME
207-624-6410

Child Labor Division
Maryland Department of Labor
MD
301-333-4193

Executive Office of Labor
Dept. of Labor and Industries
MA
617-727-6573

Bureau of Employment Standards
Michigan State Department of Labor
MI
517-322-1829

Labor Standards Division
Minnesota Dept. of Labor and Industry
MN
612-297-2225

Wage and Hour Board
Mississippi Board of Health
MS
601-965-4347

Division of Labor Standards
Missouri Labor Division
MO
314-751-3403

Employment Relations-Wage and Hour
Montana Department of Labor and Industry
MT
406-444-4665

Labor and Safety Standards
Dept. of Labor, Division of Safety
NE
402-595-3095

Capitol Complex
Nevada Dept. of Industry Relations
NV
702-687-4850

Inspection Div./Wage & Hour
New Hampshire Dept. of Labor
NH
603-271-2597

Office of Wage and Hour Compliance
New Jersey Dept. of Labor
NJ
609-292-7860

New Mexico State Dept. of Labor
NM
505-827-6830

Div. of Labor Standards
New York State Dept. of Labor
NY
518-457-2460

Wage & Hour Div.
North Carolina Dept. of Labor
NC
919-733-0358

North Dakota Dept. of Labor
ND
701-224-2660

Prevailing Wage, Minimum Wage, Minors
Ohio Dept. of Industrial Relations
OH
614-644-2239

Oklahoma State Dept. of Labor
OK
405-528-1500

Oregon Bureau of Labor & Industries
OR
503-229-6486

Bureau of Labor Standards
Pennsylvania State Dept. of Labor
PA
717-787-4670

Bureau of Labor Standards
Puerto Rico Dept. of Labor
PR
809-754-5810

Div. of Labor Standards
Rhode Island State Dept. of Labor
RI
401-457-1808

Public Information
South Carolina Dept. of Labor
SC
803-734-9688

Office of the Secretary
South Dakota State Dept. of Labor
SD
605-773-3682

Div. of Labor Standards
Tennessee State Dept. of Labor
TN
615-741-2858

Texas State Dept. of Health
TX
512-463-3173

Utah Industrial Commission
UT
801-530-6880

Wage & Hour Division
Vermont Dept. of Labor & Industry
VT
802-828-2157

Virgin Islands Dept. of Labor - Safety
809-773-1994

Div. of State Labor Law Administration
Virginia State Dept. of Labor
VA
804-786-3224

Dept. of Labor & Industries
Washington State Dept. of Labor
WA
206-753-3487

Wage & Hour Div.
West Virginia State Dept. of Labor
WV
304-558-7890

Equal Rights Division
Wisconsin State Dept. of Labor
WI
608-266-0026

Child Labor Commission
Wyoming State Dept. of Labor
WY
307-777-7261

CHAPTER 12

Who We Are & How We Do It

WHO WE ARE AND HOW WE DO IT

WHAT IS THE COUNCIL ON ECONOMIC PRIORITIES?

When Alice Tepper Marlin founded the Council on Economic Priorities in 1969, few corporations felt responsible for the environment or fair employment.

Today, that attitude has changed. CEP and our members have helped change it.

CEP has gathered and documented facts in more than 1,000 publications, major studies and research reports on child care, air pollution, occupational safety, the politics of defense contracting, and converting to a peace economy.

CEP's goal is to inform the American public and inspire corporations to be good citizens, responsive to the social concerns of all their employees, neighbors, investors, and consumers.

Our recent books include: *Shopping for a Better World: A Quick and Easy Guide to Socially Responsible Supermarket Shopping* (Ballantine, 1992), which rates the social records of 166 consumer products companies whose products you might buy when you go grocery shopping. In 1994, we plan to publish *The Comprehensive Shopping for a Better World*, which will include cars, appliances, computers, clothes, and toys, as well as the food and other consumer products already covered in the supermarket edition. CEP's SCREEN service provides social responsibility information to investors, so that they can "screen" their portfolios. Our Corporate Environmental Data Clearinghouse offers in-depth analyses of the environmental performance of companies.

CEP launched a new campaign in 1992 called the Campaign for Cleaner Corporations. This new research project names eight of the worst companies for the environment in industries including aerospace, automotive, building, and oil and calls for specific reforms. Joining CEP in this campaign is a coalition of activist groups including the Rainforest Action Network, the National Toxics Campaign, and the Student Environmental Action Coalition. The eight companies cited were Cargill, Du Pont, General Electric, General Motors, Georgia Pacific, Maxxam, Rockwell, and USX.

CEP is an independent, nonprofit public interest research organization supported by a nationwide membership and by individual and foundation grants. You can join. You'll receive a free updated copy of ***Shopping For a Better World*** every year and the CEP newsletter every month. You'll also be entitled to a 20% discount on our in-depth, company environmental reports and all our books. To join, please send in the order form at the back of this book.

ABOUT THE RESEARCH

The Council on Economic Priorities gathered information from a variety of sources:

1) questionnaires filled out by the companies themselves;
2) printed material from, or phone interviews with, company officials;
3) specialized institutions such as the American Committee on Africa, Animal Rights International, Black Enterprise, Center for Science in the Public Interest, Citizens for a Better Environment, Corporate Crime Reporter, the Data Center, Earth Island Institute, Environmental Defense Fund, Environmental Law Institute, Foundation Center, Franklin Research and Development, Friends of the Earth, Greenpeace, The Humane Society of the United States, Interfaith Center on Corporate Responsibility, Investor Responsibility Research Center, Johns Hopkins Center for Alternatives to Animal Testing, National Association for the Advancement of Colored

People, National Boycott News, National Toxics Campaign, National Women's Economic Alliance Foundation, the Natural Resources Defense Council, New Consumer, Nuclear Information and Resource Service, Organic Foods Production Association of North America, Renew America, Rainforest Action Network, Sierra Club Legal Defense Fund, United Nations Environment Program, Working Committee on Community Right to Know, Worldwatch Institute;

4) business and public libraries, especially for such resources as Taft Corporate Giving Directory, National Data Book, Monthly Labor Review, Bureau of National Affairs publications, Nexis and Lexis;

5) U.S. government agencies such as the Bureau of Labor Statistics, the Environmental Protection Agency, Occupational Safety and Health Administration, Department of Agriculture, Small Business Administration, the National Labor Relations Board, and state and regional regulatory agencies;

6) advisers who are experts in our various categories.

After months of research, we sent each company our ratings with a request for corrections and updates.

The Council looks for comprehensive, comparable data, a task that is far more difficult in some areas than in others. For example, definitive data is publicly available on South African involvement, making this issue easier to compare. A category such as the environment is extremely complex. Data were not always comparable company-to-company or year to year. Foreign companies especially do not always present comparable data. Our ability to obtain and verify data is much stronger for the domestic operations of U.S. companies.

Where firms cooperated with CEP's efforts by answering all or most of our survey, a more complete picture emerges. CEP thanks the cooperating companies for providing us with comprehensive information.

ADVISERS

These are all the people who helped us with the book, by giving us feedback, suggestions, criticism, or information about companies or issues. To each one we say thanks—a lot!

THE TEENS:

Dana Armstrong
Richmond, IN

Marina Banje
Irvington, NY

Lew Breckenridge
Waterville, KS

Brandi Bruns
College Corner, OH

John Buchanan
Sherman, TX

Gillian Chi
Brooklyn, NY

Andy Cook
Tyler, TX

Erica Cummings
Palestine, TX

Amber Davis
Newcastle, OK

Emily Gold
Irvington, NY

Kathy Hanman
Bourbon, IN

Leah Hickey
Berkeley, CA

Brett Hilsabeck
Wills Point, TX

Wendy Kraus
Phoenix, AZ

Tara Lee
Newcastle, OK

Amanda Manuel
Palestine, TX

Patrick Martin
Richmond, IN

Nicola McClung
Berkeley, CA

Louisa Michaels
Berkeley, CA

Kyle Munigle
Irvington, NY

Matthew Paice
New York, NY

Kim Palmer
Bethesda, MD

Nathan Parsley
Berkeley, CA

Michelle Quick
Bourbon, IN

Nancy Reyes
Richmond Hill, NY

Sean Rinzler
Woodstock, NY

Sarah Robart
Rockville, MD

Ocean Robbins
Santa Cruz, CA

Jennifer Rubenstein
Pittsford, NY

Karina Sang
Bronx, NY

Katie Shein
Hightstown, NJ

Lisa Shilvock
Tyler, TX

Renee Sinkfield
Petersburg, VA

Ben Spinella
Irvington, NY

Amanda Stafford
Argos, IN

Jason Topel
Irvington, NY

Sasha Waldrep
Troup, TX

Christina Weise
Tyler, TX

Mandy Weldy
Etna Green, IN

Gabby Zeitchick
Tarrytown, NY

JUNIOR HIGH, HIGH SCHOOL, AND COLLEGE TEACHERS:

Ava Mendelson
Theresa Phillips
Carolyn Ramey
Charlotte Schuur
Deborah Stone
Alecia Wolf
Linda Young

OTHER EXPERTS:

Jon Berry
Author
How to Market to Kids

Phil Catalfo
Co-author
50 Simple Things Kids Can Do to Save the Earth

Bill DeRosa
Youth Education Division
Humane Society of the US

Yvonne Finnie
Youth and College Division
NAACP

Carol Glade
National Coalition for Consumer Education

Linda Golodner
Executive Director
National Consumers League

Philip Kay
Editor
New Youth Connections

Vanessa Kirsch
Public Allies: National Center for Careers in Public Life

Matt Nicodemus
Good Work!

Jane Rinzler
Author
Teens Speak Out

Skip Sturman
Career Works

RATINGS ADVISERS

Melanie Adcock
Director, Farm Animals
Humane Society of the US

Mark Albion
Chairman
Applebrook Farms

Dorianne Beyer
General Counsel
National Child Labor Committee

Simon Billenness, Patrick McVeigh
Franklin Research and Development

James S. Cannon
President
Energy Futures, Inc.

Jennifer Davis
Executive Director
American Committee on Africa

Jerome Dodson
President
The Parnassus Fund

Terry Gips
President
International Alliance for Sustainable Agriculture

Kathy Guillermo
Director, Caring Consumer Campaign
People for the Ethical Treatment of Animals

Michael Jacobson, Ph.D.
Executive Director
Center for Science in the Public Interest

Chuck Johnson
Executive Director
Nuclear Free America

Richard Knight
Executive Director
New Consumer

Howard Lyman
Executive Director
Beyond Beef Campaign

Joel Makower
Editor-in-Chief
Tilden Press, The Green Consumer Letter

Jim Mason
Author
Animal Factories

Susan Meeker-Lowry
Director
Catalyst

Keith Mestrich
Director of Special Services
Food and Allied Service Trades Dept. AFL-CIO

Ruth Ruttenberg
Ruttenberg Associates

Tim Smith
Executive Director
Interfaith Center on Corporate Responsibility

Henry Spira
President
Animal Rights International

Ann Taylor
Administrator, Fair Share Program
NAACP

Peter Webster
Director
Ethical Investment Research Service

CRITERIA COMMITTEE, CEP BOARD OF DIRECTORS:

John T. Connor Jr.
Anne S. Davidson
Joseph W. Garton
Albert C. Hurwit
Jacob Imberman
Beth Smith
George Wallerstein

BRANDNAME INDEX

PRODUCT INDEX

SURVEY

This book was written with the help of students like you, and we need your help to make future editions of **STUDENTS SHOPPING FOR A BETTER WORLD** even better!

So please take a minute to answer the following questions, tear the pages out and send them to CEP, 30 Irving Place, New York, NY 10003.

1. Have you changed any products you buy because of a product's rating in **STUDENTS SHOPPING FOR A BETTER WORLD?**

☐ Yes ☐ No

If yes, please give an example of which product and why.

2. What companies, products or brands not listed in **STUDENTS SHOPPING FOR A BETTER WORLD** would you like to see listed in future editions? PLEASE SPECIFY:

____________________ ____________________

____________________ ____________________

____________________ ____________________

3. CEP rated companies on four social issues. How important are these issues to you? Please rank them 1 - 4, with 1 being the most important.

- ☐ Disclosure of information
- ☐ Environment
- ☐ Minority Advancement
- ☐ Women's Advancement

4. Would you like us to rate companies on these issues?

	Yes	No
Charitable Giving	☐	☐
Community Outreach (Investing in low income housing, employee volunteer programs, etc.)	☐	☐
Family Benefits (child care, flex-time, etc.)	☐	☐
Workplace Issues (occupational health & safety, pensions, etc.)	☐	☐
Sustainable development in developing countries.	☐	☐

5. How often do you take a company's rating into account when you decide to buy a company's product?

- ☐ All the time
- ☐ Regularly
- ☐ Occasionally
- ☐ Seldom
- ☐ Never

6. Have you written to a company as a result of reading this book?

☐ Yes ☐ No

7. This book has chapters on advertising, social action, etc. Did you read these chapters?

☐ Yes ☐ No

If yes, check the chapters that you liked the most.

☐ Who Cares? You Care!
☐ Your Job/ Your Career
☐ Shopping For A Better Environment
☐ Social Action
☐ All About Advertising
☐ It's in Your Hands
☐ Money Matters

8. How did you hear about **STUDENTS SHOPPING FOR A BETTER WORLD** ?

☐ a friend
☐ newspaper
☐ family member
☐ magazine
☐ school
☐ TV
☐ camp/religious group
☐ radio
☐ membership organization
☐ bookstore
☐ CEP member
☐ other

9. How interested would you (or someone in yout family) be in the following guides?

	Very Interested	Somewhat Interested	Not Interested
Kids (and Parents) for ages 0-10	☐	☐	☐
Shopping for a Better Place to Work	☐	☐	☐
Senior Citizens	☐	☐	☐
Comprehensive Consumer Products (appliances, cars, electronics, etc.)	☐	☐	☐

10. How old are you?

☐ 11 or younger
☐ 12 - 14
☐ 15 - 17
☐ 18 - 21
☐ Over 21

11. Any other comments/suggestions on **STUDENTS SHOPPING FOR A BETTER WORLD ?**

____

____

____

____

Thank You!

A TEACHER'S GUIDE TO STUDENTS SHOPPING FOR A BETTER WORLD

Let *A Teacher's Guide to Students Shopping For A Better World* by Professor William D. Coplin and Tara Kneller (Policy Studies Associates 1993) help you introduce your students to the philosophy of corporate social responsibility.

The guide is an exciting tool for sharpening students' research and decision-making skills. It provides materials designed to stimulate class discussion and exercises on how to use *Students Shopping For A Better World* in everyday economic decisions, how to conduct a study of a corporation or local business, how to influence corporations to adopt socially responsible policies and more.

William D. Coplin is Professor of Public Affairs at the Maxwell School of Syracuse University. Tara Kneller is the founder and president of Futures, a student organization at Syracuse University.

A Teacher's Guide to Students Shopping For A Better World is available to educators and CEP members at $23.00 (includes shipping and handling). A free Mother Jones *Students Shopping For A Better World* poster is included with each order.

Teachers who purchase the guide may also purchase copies of *Students Shopping For A Better World* for classroom use at special discount rates.

To place your order or for more information, please use the coupon or call CEP at 1-800-729-4237 or (212) 420-1133.

☐ YES, please send me **A Teacher's Guide To Students Shopping For A Better World** and my free Mother Jones poster.

☐ Copies of **A Teacher's Guide to Students Shopping For A Better World** (educators and CEP members) @ $23.00 each.

☐ Send me discount rate information for **Students Shopping For A Better World.**

Name ______________________________
School's Name (educators only) ______________
Address ____________________________
City _____________ State _____ Zip ______
Phone (___) ________________________

Visa/MC/Amex ________________________
Exp. Signature ________________________

FOREIGN ORDERS: Please add $10. Payment in US dollars only.

Please send this coupon with your check or credit card information to CEP, 30 Irving Place, New York, NY 10003. Or call us at 1-800-729-4237 (420-1133 in New York City).

SBWT

GREAT BUYS FOR STUDENTS WHO CARE

Students Shopping For A Better World Poster
Post your principles with the official Mother Jones *Students Shopping For A Better World* poster. Colorful graphics + recycled paper = the socially responsible way to decorate your room. A bargain at only $5.00, it's yours free when you become a member of CEP. $5.00/free for CEP members. ITEM PST.

Shopping For A Better World - Software Version
The quick and easy supermarket shopping guide just got quicker and easier! Create your own personal shopping list in seconds. Write to companies using time-saving mail-merge features. And software comes in environmentally sound packaging. $39.00/$31.00 for CEP members. ITEM SBW9.

Shopping For A Better World Canvas Bag
Cut down on wasteful disposable shopping bags when you use this durable, lightweight canvas bag with the *Shopping For A Better World* logo. Carrying capacity is larger than a brown paper grocery bag. $11.95/$9.95 for CEP members. ITEM CVS.

Cotton String Bag
Folds up to fit in your pocket and expands to carry about as much as a regular grocery bag. $5.00, two for $8.95/$4.00 each for CEP members. ITEM STR.

To order, simply fill out the attached membership/order form and mail it with your payment to: CEP, 30 Irving Place, New York, NY 10003. Or call 1-800-729-4237 (420-1133 in New York City).

FREE

Readers of **STUDENTS SHOPPING FOR A BETTER WORLD** can receive FREE INFORMATION.

To receive any of the free information below, please fill out this form and mail it to CEP, 30 Irving Place, New York, NY 10003.

- ☐ Free CEP *Research Report* on:
  - ☐ A Guide for Social Investors
  - ☐ The Forest Products Industry
  - ☐ 1993 America's Corporate Conscience Award Winners
- ☐ More information about CEP.
- ☐ More information on CEP's Corporate Environmental Data Clearinghouse (CEDC).
- ☐ Information on SCREEN, CEP's research service for institutional investors.
- ☐ Information on quantity discounts for **STUDENTS SHOPPING FOR A BETTER WORLD** and/or **SHOPPING FOR A BETTER WORLD: A Quick and Easy Guide to Socially Responsible Supermarket Shopping.**

Name ____________________

Address ____________________

City ____________________

State ________ Zip______ Phone ____________

Please send information about CEP and **STUDENTS SHOPPING FOR A BETTER WORLD** to my friend(s):

Name(s) ____________________

Address(es) ____________________

____

NOR3

Who Says You Can't Change the World?

CEP is an independent, nonprofit public research organization supported by people like you. Our goal is to inform the American public and inspire corporations to be good citizens responsive to social concerns.

With the help of our members, CEP created STUDENTS SHOPPING FOR A BETTER WORLD. With your help, CEP can continue to launch new projects and convince America's corporations to be more socially responsible.

When you become a member of CEP, you join thousands of other concerned citizens who believe we can change the world. All members receive monthly fact-filled Research Reports, a free copy of CEP's latest Shopping Guide each year, a 20% discount on all CEP books and studies, and a free STUDENTS SHOPPING FOR A BETTER WORLD poster.

So join CEP today! Simply fill out the reverse side of this page and mail it with your tax-deductible contribution.

*$25/year: Regular Member.

Students pay only $20—supported by a $5 "scholarship" from CEP!

*$100/year: Donor—Receive all CEP books and studies released in that year.

*$250/year: Sponsor—All the above plus a free in-depth report on any company we are currently tracking.

*$500/year: Patron—All the above plus first class mailing of monthly Research Report, annual listing in Research Report and an invitation to Executive Director's Reception at our America's Corporate Conscience Awards (ACCA).

*$1,000/year: Director's Circle—All the above plus reserved seating with CEP Director at America's Corporate Conscience Awards and a listing in our annual report.

MEMBERSHIP/ORDER FORM ON REVERSE SIDE

CEP MEMBERSHIP/ORDER FORM

☐ Yes, I want to help change the world! Enroll me as a CEP member today and welcome me with a free STUDENTS SHOPPING FOR A BETTER WORLD poster.

☐ $25* ☐ $100 ☐ $250 ☐ $500 ☐ $1,000 ☐ $____

*Students pay $20 and receive a $5 "scholarship" to join CEP!

☐ And please send me the following CEP publications and products:

______ copies of STUDENTS SHOPPING FOR A BETTER WORLD @ $7.49 or five copies for $23.95

______ copies of SHOPPING FOR A BETTER WORLD: A Quick and Easy Guide to Socially Responsible Supermarket Shopping @ $7.49 or five copies for $23.95.

☐ Other ______________________________

☐ Other ______________________________

Name ______________________________

Address ______________________________

City ______________ State ______ Zip __________

Visa/MC/Amex ______________________________

Exp. Date ________ Signature ______________________

FOREIGN ORDERS: Please add $10. Payment in US dollars only.

Please send this form with your check or credit card information to CEP, 30 Irving Place, New York, NY 10003. Or call us at 1-800-729-4237 (420-1133 in New York City). Your membership contribution (less the value of any premium you receive) is tax-deductible.

PRIVILEGES OF MEMBERSHIP ON REVERSE SIDE

BAL3